T.J. Rohleder Brings You...

The Ruthless Marketing Attack!

Greetings, Future Ruthless Marketer!

My name is T.J. Rohleder, and **I'm here to help you make more money than you ever dreamed possible**.

Does that sound too good to be true? Well, maybe it is, if you want the world handed to you on a silver platter. **But the flat-out truth is that the marketing system about which you will learn about in this book has the potential to make you literally millions of dollars – if you're willing to work for it.**

I'm living proof!

My wife and I started out with just $300 nineteen years ago, and we've built that into a marketing empire that has brought in more than $110 million today. Hey, if it can happen to a couple of little Forrest Gumps like us from small-town America, it can happen to anyone. I honestly believe this is true because, after all, I've lived it! Now, I'm not going to fool you. It took a lot of hard work to get there. **But, I'm convinced that anybody willing to put in the effort can succeed like we did, <u>as long as they apply these marketing techniques to their business</u>.** The best part is, there's plenty of room for everyone up here at the top.

The book you're reading now grew out of the original Ruthless Marketing Attack Workshop we held in Goessel, Kansas. In attendance were several of the greatest names in the modern marketing field, people that I'm proud to call my friends.

My colleagues Chris Lakey, Chris Hollinger, and John Alanis joined me to talk about the ruthless marketing techniques that have earned us millions upon millions of dollars, and the text you're about to read evolved from the give-and-take between our panel members and our seminar audience.

The harvest of advanced, effective, and above all ruthless marketing techniques I'll present to you in the upcoming chapters can set you on the road to earning all the money you've ever dreamed of – as long as you don't hesitate to use them, as so many people do. **I guarantee you: all it takes is a little elbow grease, and you'll be on your way to the top!**

TABLE OF CONTENTS

INTRODUCTION

"What Ruthless Means to Me"

The system I'm going to teach you in this book is called Ruthless Marketing. I know that sounds somewhat coldblooded, so I thought I'd start off by telling you exactly why I chose that name for both the system and the title of this book.

At first, it doesn't seem like the most charming title, especially given the word with which I started. If you look up its primary definition, "ruthless" isn't a good word at all; it's actually pretty terrible. It describes people who can hurt others without any remorse, or who can inflict pain on somebody else without it bothering them. Sociopaths and psychopaths, in other words.

But that's not what I'm trying to convey here. The English language is constantly evolving, and "ruthless" has more subtle, less-offensive meanings than the one mentioned above. The meaning of "ruthless" I chose for this system is, well, less ruthless than the official meaning. It's closer to "aggressive" or "assertive" than anything else. **With this kind of ruthlessness, you're being proactive by taking your success into your own hands.** You're not just waiting for things to happen; you're out there making things happen. "Ruthless" is a great marketing term because it paints a word picture in your mind. Think of somebody who's "aggressive." Get a word picture? Not so much. "Assertive?" Even weaker. How about "ruthless"? That's it. **If you want to sell something to somebody, you need to engage**

their mind first.

I could just as accurately have called this book *Aggressive Marketing Attack* – but it doesn't sound as catchy, does it? It's not as dramatic. **It's not as marketable.** And therein lies the heart of the system: marketing. If you ask a hundred different experts what "marketing" means, you're going to get a hundred different definitions. A college business professor might talk your ear off for 10 or 20 minutes about the definition of marketing, and you won't even understand half of what they're saying. **But my definition of marketing is simple: it's all the things you do in your business to attract and then sell to the right people, the ones who are perfectly suited for whatever it is you're selling.**

And then there's the third word in the title. What does "attack" mean to you? When I studied that word, I saw plenty of negative definitions. It's a very aggressive word. But whenever I do word studies, I always look at its antonym – that is, the opposite of that particular word. It turns out that the opposite of attack is defend. **There's a certain mindset involved in the act of defending, whether in warfare or in marketing, and there's another involved in the act of attacking.** Again, we encounter words like offensive, proactive, assertive, aggressive.

So think about the whole idea behind the name of this product: "*Ruthless Marketing Attack.*" Think of it as something that's offensive, in the best sense of the word, rather than defensive. It's the opposite of passive. That's beneficial to you as a marketer, and do you know why? **Because most business people are unbelievably passive, and you can easily take advantage of their passivity in order to profit.**

I can best define this with a story, which comes from my friend and mentor Russ von Hoelscher. Russ is the man who helped us become millionaires back in the late 1980s; he was the guy who taught us the secrets of effective marketing. Russ used to have (and note that I say used to have) one printer who did all his printing. Russ is a marketing guy, so he was constantly giving his printer all kinds of marketing advice, saying stuff like, "Look, John, you ought to do this and this and this to promote your printing business." But John's answer was always the same: **"Russ, if they want printing, they know where to come."** He had a little sign up in front of his shop and figured that would bring him all the work he needed.

Have you ever seen the movie Field of Dreams, with Kevin Costner? The whole message of that movie was, **"If you build it – they will come."**

Most business owners have adopted that mentality as their own. **It's a passive kind of thing; they're just sitting back, waiting for people to come to them, hoping the market's going to improve, hoping things are going to change**. They're blaming everybody and everything for their circumstances: the economy, the competition, roadwork, maybe the weather. Life gets hard, and the first time they face major adversity they give up. **That mindset is the opposite of the mindset I'm planning to drill into your head with this book**. Think of it as "Passive Marketing Acceptance," as opposed to what you'll be learning here.

Their mindset is good news for you, though, because if you can be ruthless in the right way, you're going to grab their business away from them. You'll be one of those factors they're complaining about, instead of doing something about. **If there's one thing I want you to take away from this book, it's the confidence of knowing that if you choose to use the ideas and methods that I'll be sharing with you, you have a major advantage over most of the business people out there**. And when I say "most," I'm talking about as many as 80-90% of the people selling in your market: the folks who do things in a haphazard, weak, and ineffective way.

Early this morning, I cracked open one of my favorite quote books, and here's the quote that hit me: **"The uncommitted life isn't worth living."** It's a quote from 1963 by a man named Marshall Fishwick. That's a heck of a thing to have hit you at six AM, but I thought it was appropriate. When I think of good marketers – the ones that I respect, the ones from whom I take my cues – I find that they're deeply committed. **There's nothing that's going to stop these guys.** They face all kinds of adversity, they keep getting knocked down, and they keep getting up over and over again. No matter how bad things get, they ain't quitting! And because they refuse to quit, they never lose.

I know that that sounds simplistic, like something you'd get out of some cheesy self-help book, but it's true. These marketers are in it with all their hearts. **They refuse to quit – and because they refuse to quit, they can't be beaten.** If they keep pushing and keep learning and keep expanding, they eventually develop the knowledge, skills, and experience that take them to the top. And then, of course, everybody says that they got lucky – but that's another story.

The Truth About Talent

There's a show business adage that says, "Talent rises to the top." I believe that's true to some extent, but I also believe something else: **<u>I believe we have it within ourselves to create our own talent.</u>**

A while back, my granddaughter was over at my house. She plays her dad's drums sometimes, and she was telling me that she has absolutely no talent at it. Those were her actual words: an 11-year-old girl told me, "I have absolutely no talent." I told her, "Honey, if you stick with it long enough, you'll

---

develop your talent." **I honestly believe that if you want something bad enough, and you're willing to pay the price and do whatever it takes to get it, eventually you'll develop the necessary ingredients – the knowledge, the skills, and the experience – to take you to the top.**

Take my company, for example. We've worked our tails off and have striven to develop our talent over the course of almost twenty years, and **so far we've earned over $113 million in sales in our first 19 years**. I'm not telling you this to brag, (okay, maybe a little!), but my point is that <u>you really can develop your talent and make loads of money if you just keep trying</u>. That's my definition of talent: not knowing when to quit. In fact, some would say that's my biggest talent, period.

You don't go from $0 to $113 million in 19 years, by doing the opposite of Ruthless Marketing. You have to be aggressive in the marketplace. You have to go out there and do everything within your power – legally, morally, ethically – to get as much of the market share as you can. **It doesn't matter what your business is, what your products or services are, or to whom you're selling**. It's all about being aggressive in your marketplace and attempting to get as many dollars as you can out of that marketplace.

My friend and colleague Chris Lakey defines *Ruthless Marketing Attack* as "the offensive-minded battle that is waged in the marketplace over who gets the largest share of your market's disposable income." <u>Marketing sissies need not enter the game</u>.

When I was a kid I watched a few of those pro-wrestling survivor matches – you know, where they start with something like 30 wrestlers in the ring, and the goal is to be the last one standing. **Just about anything goes in that kind of match**, and the goal is to get the other guys out of the ring and onto the floor of the arena. They can be hanging on the ropes, or over the side of the ring, and that's okay; but once they hit the floor they're out.

That's what *Ruthless Marketing Attack* is all about: kicking the other guys in your marketplace out of the ring. **Within certain moral, ethical, and legal boundaries, your business is in a fight for survival.** It's do or die. Darwin's theory was survival of the fittest, but in business it's survival of the fattest – fattest bank account, that is! There are hundreds of millions of dollars being spent every year on all kinds of non-essential products and services. **Don't let people tell you they don't have money because they've got it.** We're the richest nation in the world, and people have money. It's just a matter of whether they're spending it with you or with one of your competitors. You've got to learn to attract their attention, to stay in there and take the money that could and should be yours. In large part, that's what talent is, in business or in life: pure tenacity, the will to stick to it and learn to do what needs to be done in order to survive and thrive.

Let me reemphasize that all the money that you want is out there waiting for you right now, in the pockets, purses, bank accounts, and credit card authorizations of millions of people who've been fragmented into smaller and smaller niche markets as our society becomes increasingly technological and complex. It can be hard to get to, sure, because nowadays there are now niches within niches within niches. But this is a good thing! It gives the average entrepreneur like you and me, the person who wasn't born with a silver spoon in his mouth, the chance to use their intelligence and persistence to tease out a fortune from a market that might not have existed yesterday. **The average person has more chances today to make millions of dollars than ever before, just by serving these small niche markets**.

That can require some hard work, but it can often

The Ruthless Marketing Attack!

generate obscene profits – the kind of money you'd never make in a regular job, even by working overtime and getting double time on holidays. **You can work when you want, as much as you want, and dress any way you want to**. That's the kind of power that having your own business can give you – and why else would you start your own business? Admittedly, you sometimes have to scramble and reassess your business, especially if the market changes. It's always a challenge because, since the can be so fickle, what works today might not work tomorrow. **But the principles of Ruthless Marketing – whether you're selling information, opportunity, products, or services – are applicable to just about any market, and any business.** And remember: the right idea, just one little idea, can make you a million dollars.

Case in point: my colleague Chris Hollinger was recently talking about a sandwich shop that had opened up near his house. Ironically, the name of the shop was T.J.'s Deli! He'd go in there and see how they were doing, and they always seemed to be hurting for a little business. Once he became a "regular," he started giving them some ideas about how they could advertise. Chris noticed that that they had some very attractive young ladies working there, and suggested something he'd heard Russ von Hoelscher recommend for another sandwich shop in San Diego. Russ told the owner of that place, "Take these young girls you have working here, give them some samples of sandwiches, and have them go to these office complexes and pass out these sandwiches. It will get your business going!"

When Chris made the same suggestion to the folks at his local sandwich shop, the owner said, "Well, I don't know about that," but Chris said, "Trust me; it will work." They may or may not have done what Chris suggested, but a couple days later Chris drove by and saw one of those nice-looking girls out on the street with a sign that said "T.J. needs your business!" **And the**

---

parking lot was full at lunchtime. So maybe Chris gave him an idea that will eventually earn the owner that million bucks.

The Zen of Ruthless Marketing

As you read this book, I want you to keep in mind these basic facts: **the secret to effectively making money in the marketing field is to find a niche, stubbornly develop that niche, and be ruthless in exploiting it in every legal, ethical, and moral way possible**. Can you be a ruthless, nice guy? Sure, as long as you're not nice to the wrong people – that is, your competitors. But you can make even them respect you. While being ruthless can have negative connotations in the business world, it does have a component that's very much admired: a relentlessness that people respect because the ruthless person is firm in their purpose and they never, never stop.

Ruthlessness is a mindset that you have to develop in order to make it and survive and prosper in business. **The reason is this: if you have a ruthless marketing mindset, you understand that the only activity that produces revenue in your business is marketing: communicating with your customers to get them to buy more from you, or to improve your relationship with your customer so that they will continue to buy from you in the future.**

Russ von Hoelscher's former printer is a perfect example of somebody who didn't understand why this is so important. He thought his business was about the printing. But business is not about the making of the thing, the delivering of the thing, or the hiring of the employees to manage the thing. **The only activity in your business that produces revenue is marketing**. As a business owner, marketing is the highest-value task you can do. When you adopt this ruthless marketing mindset, that's the thing that will carry you forward. **If you get caught up in the** minutia of the accounting and the customer service and the shipping – things that other people are much better at doing – and you don't do the marketing, then <u>your business will collapse</u>. Period.

A ruthless marketing mindset orients you to the fact that you've got to be using your time on the only thing that produces revenue in your business, which is marketing. And you have to be ruthless with yourself about that! <u>You have to be relentless with yourself</u>! You have to be aggressive about it on a day-to-day basis. Because if you're not, your revenue is going to dry up and you're going to end up being a passive pushover. That's no good because those guys go broke! So study the steps I've outlined in this book, chapter by chapter, take some notes, and apply what works to your business. **Get sufficiently ruthless, and <u>I guarantee</u> you'll see a difference in your income in less time than you thought possible.**

CHAPTER ONE

"Practice, Practice, Practice!"

Here's an old joke you've probably heard. A tourist asks a New Yorker how to get to Carnegie Hall, and of course the New Yorker pops off, "Practice, practice, practice!"

That's particularly applicable to Ruthless Marketing because, hey, how do you become a powerful, results-getting marketer? **Practice, practice, practice!**

The truth is, in many cases what we call talent is a manifestation of the willingness to work hard and enhance a natural tendency, however small, that already exists. The great horror writer Stephen King said it best: "When I talk about my craft, I emphasize one point over and over again. You don't have to be great to do a thing, you just have to not get tired of trying to be good at it."

I think that's incredibly important because, too often, people think they have to be perfect to get started in business, that they have to have everything figured out, with all the T's crossed and all the I's dotted. **But, if you wait until you have everything all laid out and ready to go before you ever get started, you may very well be shooting yourself in the foot**, especially if you're a perfectionist for whom it's very, very hard to get everything right to your satisfaction.

In the introduction, I mentioned my 11-year-old granddaughter, who contends that she has absolutely no talent at playing the drums – although she's just a kid, and hasn't really tried hard yet. Now, the same little girl loves to dance, and she goes to a dance class once a week. Recently her dance instructor sent her Mom an email. She said, first of all, that my granddaughter was really good at dancing, and that she has a natural talent for it. She went onto say she's at the point where if she wants to take it to the next level, she needs to attend classes more than once a week and needs to practice more.

So if she wants to amplify that talent, it's going to cost more time and money every week. Is she serious about wanting to take it to the next level? That's up to her; the last I heard, no decision had been made. But if she does want to get better, she has to try to be good at it. It's not like playing the drums. She doesn't really care much about that, except every once in a while when she thinks about it, so she's not going to try to be good at it and probably never will be.

It's the same thing with marketing. If you want to be a good marketer, you don't have to be great when you get started. But you do have to be committed to trying to be good at it. **You have to be committed to doing all the things it takes to be good**. That means studying marketers and attending workshops. It means buying books or borrowing them from the library.

It means consistently buying information products from other people. It means hanging out with people who are good marketers. You have to try to be good at it; not great, just good. <u>If you commit yourself to trying to be good, you'll eventually get there by default</u>. You'll become a great marketer because you'll study everyday and come to know great marketing at a glance. **It will become a part of who you are, how you act, and how you think.**

In contrast, you'll always be terrible at marketing if you don't try to get better at it because, obviously, you're not committed to trying; in fact, you're committed to not trying. <u>You can't just sit there and hope it'll come to you</u>. **Either you're**

moving forward, trying to get better – or you're not trying, so you're moving backwards and getting worse. As Stephen King might put it, you have to not get tired of trying to be good at marketing.

A quick but constructive aside here, given the subject of this book. It's funny, but what came to mind as I related the story about my granddaughter and the dance lessons was the fact that the instructor probably has a stock email, and this is part of their reselling technique.

They send the email to the proud parents saying, "'Insert Name Here' is very good at dancing, and blah blah blah." **The point is, the instructor's pushing an up-sell here, "The next step is, your daughter needs more lessons."** It's an example of good marketing in practice. Like the web sites that tell you, "Click here for a coupon," or those poetry contests you see in the back of magazines. Most writers and would-be poets have fallen for those things! They've been running those "Poets Wanted" ads for God knows how long, and you could just put some dumb little thing together, no matter what it is, and submit it – and they'll send you a letter saying, "You are the next great writer!" Of course they'll tell you they want to publish your poem in this or that book, and ask you to buy a copy in advance. **Now, do you think they'll publish your little ditty if you don't buy a copy for yourself, your Mom, your grandma, and your Great-Aunt Ethel?** Of course they won't. Those are some ruthless marketers, I tell you! But if you do buy, you can count on getting that poem in print.

But, back to practicing your marketing! **You absolutely have to stick with it, and anyone can learn how to do this, as long as you believe in yourself.** Take my friend and colleague Chris Hollinger, who was one of the people who spoke at the Ruthless Marketing Attack seminar on which this book is based. He said at the seminar he realizes that, having gone from a teaching background to this marketplace rather suddenly, he still has a lot to learn – and that there's no way he's even scratched the surface on what he needs to learn in order to be an even better marketer. Heck, I've been doing this for over 20 years, and I still feel the same way sometimes. But what a ride; what a good time it's been so far! Sometimes you'll learn lessons the hard way and they'll cost you money, and sometimes you'll reapply that knowledge, and boom! Something will really hit for you. **But you definitely can't give up, or you'll never become the success you ought to be**. There are so many business people who aren't concentrating on the things they need to do to improve their businesses – and just sticking with it is half the battle!

The One-Eyed Man

This brings me to another of my favorite quotes, one I heard first from Dan Kennedy: "In the land of the blind, the one-eyed man is king." I love that quote because it represents marketing so well. **Most business people aren't good marketers**. And you know what that means? That if you have just one eye open while they remain willfully blind, you're going to eventually get ahead of them. It doesn't even have to be by much; just get ahead a little and you'll start reaping the benefits, and those benefits will start building on themselves. Think of it this way: have you ever heard the story about the two guys who are in the woods camping and a bear starts chasing them, and one guy stops long enough to put on his shoes? The other guy yells at him, "You idiot, that bear's going to get you! What are you doing putting on your shoes?" And the first guy replies calmly, "Look, I don't have to run faster than the bear. I just have to run faster than you!"

So you only have to be a bit better than everyone else to start hauling in the cash. **Just a little of the knowledge I'm**

---

trying to share with you here puts you light years ahead of most people who are marketing their businesses because they're doing a really bad job. They're no longer trying to continue to be good; they're just stuck in a rut, trying to get by.

Here's another appropriate comment you should chew on: **"School is never out for the pro."** That fact should never be very far from your thoughts. Business changes so fast that you can't stay in tune with it unless you're actively and continually studying and learning all you can. I spend an ungodly amount of money every year on marketing items, money I could spend on other things. Among other things, I pay to go to seminars, to join Mastermind Groups, and to stay current with what's going on out there. **You have to, because if you don't, you're going to get left behind.**

There have been a lot of changes to our market just since we got started in 1988. For example, there was no Internet then. When you get right down to it, the Internet has hurt our market more than it helped – at least, it hurt established companies like ours, the ones that have some infrastructure. For some start-ups, of course, it's been a great thing. **That's the thing about market changes – they can help or they can hurt, depending on how you're positioned.** You have to roll with the punches and keep learning, keep practicing, or you're likely to be overcome.

Consider those start-ups I just mentioned; think about the entire personal computer industry, especially. I love reading about how all that evolved. The change happened so radically and so completely, and it's fascinating to dig into the stories behind it.

The same thing is true with the fast food industry. In a book called *McDonald's: Behind the Arches*, John F. Love writes about the rapid evolution and major challenges and struggles of the fast food industry, and it's so exciting reading about something like that – but only when it's happening to other markets. When it happens to your market, it's not exciting anymore. **If you don't stay on top of things and keep trying to be good, you'll drown.**

Which brings me back to the Stephen King quote with which I started this chapter. I consider myself a pretty good copywriter, at least within my market. However, I've been doing it for over 20 years now. Recently, we held a copywriting seminar in our facilities in Goessel, and during the course of that seminar we went over, in detail, a sales letter I had written. It took me six days to get that sales letter just the way I wanted it during the copywriting process, and we spent two full days going over it and analyzing it in excruciating detail.

At the very end of the seminar I told the attendees, "This sales letter didn't really take me six days to write. It took me 19 years and six days to write." That's very germane in this context because it's easy to look at successful entrepreneurs and think, **"They've got something on me. Somehow, they're smarter or better than me." Wrong!** <u>**They just have knowledge and experience and skills that they've developed, and that you haven't.**</u> That's all it is. Their success has been evolutionary. You may think, "Good God, I'll never be that good. I'll never have all of that." But if you do, you're shortchanging yourself. You need to realize that their skills were developed over a long period of time because those people just stuck with it long enough to finally get good at what they do.

But here's a caveat to that. **You don't have to keep working for 20 years before you get good at what you do**. Even when you're first starting out, as long as you act and apply yourself, you can write sales letters that work very well. So, you don't need 20 years when you're sincere and you're writing to the right customers, your best customers. Because if they're people with whom you have a relationship – people who have reason to like and trust you – you can be a sub-standard copywriter and still do very well. **As time passes, you'll get better and better as you go along anyway.**

You can also make some decent money if you pick the right market from the beginning, even if you're not the best writer. My colleague John Alanis considers his first sales letter to be an embarrassment because he didn't make much money in absolute terms. But consider this: his mailing cost was thirty bucks, and it brought in $150 – so that's a five-to-one return. I know a lot of professional copywriters who'd kill for those percentages. **The point is, the hotter the market, the worse you can be and still make money.**

But, no matter how hot the market is, no matter how fast the products are flying off the shelves, no matter how you relate to your customers, you can always make more money if you keep one little thing in mind: practice, practice, practice, so you can develop that little talent into a bigger one.

CHAPTER TWO

"My Story; or, a Tale of Two Men"

When I first started in business, I was in a bad place. I was broke, I was homeless, and my first business partner had just gotten out of prison. I've never told anybody this story before, but I want to tell it now because it serves a couple of points I want to make that are very important.

Think back to where you were in the summer of 1985, assuming you're old enough to remember that far back. Here's where I was: bouncing from one sales job to another. I'd been in sales for two years at that point, I didn't have a formal education, and that hurt me. I did want to make a lot of money, and the only way I could figure out how to do that was to sell stuff. So I bounced around from here to there, like so many other salespeople, going from one job to another to another.

There's a proverb from the 16th Century that says, "Little hinges swing big doors." For me, that happened when I answered an ad in a Wichita, Kansas newspaper – a tiny ad that literally changed my life. It was a "Sales Help Wanted" ad that asked for route drivers. I went to apply and found that the location of the interview was somebody's house, which I thought was kind of strange. It turned out that this young couple had just bought into a carpet cleaning franchise – Rainbow International, out of Waco, Texas.

They were looking for drivers who would go out and

work on commission and clean carpets. They'd spent all of their money, but even though they were leveraged to the hilt to buy this franchise, they were excited. They were about my age – in their early- to mid-20's – **and because they were so excited about the business, they got me excited about it, too!** Right away, I wanted to become a carpet cleaner. It was a good deal because I could keep 60% of whatever I booked – and I knew I could sell. That was my one big business talent.

The only problem was, in order to have this tremendous opportunity, I had to invest in a certain type of van on my own; they didn't have the money to provide it, and they wanted to see an act of faith on my part. So I went around and tried to get one, but I was broke, and no banker would loan me money to buy the kind of nice van they required me to get. **That's how bad my credit was**. I couldn't find anything I could afford, no matter what I did. The couple kept telling me, "Look, if you'll just get a vehicle, we'll supply the equipment."

To make a long story short, that deal fell through because I couldn't get a loan to buy that nice van I needed. But I was so sold on the idea of carpet cleaning that I went to the phone book and started calling up all the carpet cleaners in the area. I told them, "Look, I want to go to work for you on straight commission," and they all said no. I called 20 or 30 numbers before I finally found a guy in Canton, Kansas, about 30 miles from where I lived, and he said, "Okay, come out and see me. Let's talk."

So I borrowed a friend's car, because I was so broke that I didn't even have a car of my own. I was riding a bicycle, that's how broke I was. I went over there and basically sold this guy on the idea of me going to work for him. He had a Rainbow Carpet Cleaning franchise, too, which was good because I was already a little familiar with that. He had one van, and he immediately gave it to me to work with. I was out there right away, booking my own carpet cleaning jobs, getting 60% commission, and I fell in love with the business. I really liked it. He even sent me to carpet cleaning school in Waco, Texas. I was there for a couple of weeks, surrounded by all these guys who had just paid $50,000 for their franchises, and I was the only employee present. I went through all the same training they went through, even though I had to borrow the money to get on the Greyhound bus just to get to Waco. That's how poor I was in 1985. But these guys were all great. They just assumed I was a franchise owner, too, and I didn't tell them otherwise. I made some good friends, and it was a great experience.

On the way home from Waco, I got off the bus at Ark City, Kansas, and went to visit my best friend, who was in prison. His name was Gary Purvis. Gary was just getting ready to get out of prison, but I hadn't seen him for a couple years because I was living in another city when he got into trouble. Now, Gary was a great guy. I want you to know that he wasn't in prison because he was a hardened criminal; he was in prison because he was an idiot. He did the stupidest thing in the world, and it cost him 18 months of his life. I know this is going to sound crazy, but here's how it happened.

It all started because we used to fish in a little creek that runs through Newton, Kansas called Sand Creek. At the end of that creek there used to be a rubber dam, and we always fished right there at the dam. Well, there was a little hole in the rubber, and every once in a while a fish would pop out. Honest to God! We used to joke, "Hey, what are we doing fishing here? Let's just hold our net down here and we'll catch the fish as they pop out of the hole."

So one day, Gary comes up with this idea: "Well, maybe I'll just make that hole a little bigger. Then more fish will pop out, and we'll just sit here with our net and catch them without even trying." **I'm not making this up!** So he pulls out his knife and widens the hole! Was it criminal? Yes, it was, but it was mostly just stupid. The hole was already there; he just made it a little bigger, and you know what? More fish did start popping out! But the hole weakened the dam, and it collapsed. Thousands of fish died, all because of that idiotic, stupid thing my friend Gary did.

If Gary had gone right to the authorities immediately, they would have slapped him on the wrists and put him on probation – he wouldn't have spent one day behind bars. But he was stupid and tried to hide it…except he told some of his friends about it, and they told some of their friends, and nine months later the police came knocking on his door, and ultimately Gary spent 18 months in prison. It was a valuable lesson for him in the end, and I can tell you this: he'll never go back to prison again.

So there I was, fresh out of carpet cleaning school in Waco, and I stopped by to see best friend Gary, who was just about to be released. I was so excited about the carpet cleaning business, and I told him all about it – and then I hitchhiked home because I was too broke to get back on the bus!

Gary got out of prison in November 1985 and came to see me right away. It was the fall season – one of the best seasons in the carpet cleaning business – and on a good week I was bringing home a thousand a week. Of course, I had to give 40% of it to the guy in Canton, but I was making pretty good money for a guy without any skills or education, a guy who had no family to support. **And so I was waving the cash in front of Gary and, sure enough, Gary gets excited and says, "T.J., let's go into the carpet cleaning business together!"**

I swear that if it hadn't been for Gary I would have never done it because I didn't have any money to buy the equipment. Even though I was making hundreds of dollars a week, I was spending it just as fast. And at the time, I'd just broken up with a woman I'd been living with, so I was basically homeless, crashing on friends' couches, and such. I pointed all that out and Gary told me, "Don't worry, T.J., we can get all the stuff we need." And sure enough, he was right.

Not that it was easy, by any means, because by then it was December (which is the worst time you could start a carpet cleaning business). When I told all my friends and family, "I'm getting ready to start my own carpet cleaning business now," they told me, "T.J., you're a fool! First of all, your partner just got out of prison. Second of all, it's December!" Once the snow comes in Kansas, people don't want you to come in to clean their carpets.

So there were all kinds of reasons why I should have never done it; if I'd been a sane, rational, intelligent human being, there's no way on God's green Earth that I would ever have gotten in the carpet cleaning business with somebody like Gary in December, with no money, with no equipment, with no nothing.

The thing is, I didn't listen to any of those people. In Chapter 6, I'll talk about how entrepreneurship is tied to the same qualities that make some people into juvenile delinquents – at least according to Harvard business professor Abraham Zaleznik. **Those same qualities can serve us well in the world of entrepreneurialism because entrepreneurs go out there and make things happen.** They don't wait for the perfect circumstances. They take everything that could be against them and just say, **"To hell with it! I'm going to find a way to either go around it, through it, or over it."**

Both Gary and I were the entrepreneurial type, and we were entirely different from Dwayne, the man I was working for at the time. That's why I've subtitled this chapter "The Tale of Two Men," because it's a good way to contrast Dwayne and Gary.

Dwayne, my boss, was a man who grew up with money. His family owned hundreds of acres right here in Kansas, and when his parents died, they left it all to him. He spent $50,000 on this Rainbow Carpet Cleaning franchise six months before I met him. However – and this is not a put down to Dwayne, but it does serve as a good example here – what was he doing with that franchise? Nothing. The day I called him in the late summer of 1985, he was working at a factory in McPherson, Kansas, for $9 an hour, despite the fact that he'd spent $50,000 on this carpet cleaning franchise. **This is because Dwayne, although he was a nice and honest man, was also a <u>very meek and mild man</u>.** He was afraid of his own shadow, and should never have been self-employed – unless he first found a partner who had some of the qualities he lacked.

There are so many people who get into business for themselves who are like Dwayne: they lack what I call "hustle." **It's not a matter of being smart or dumb; it's just something else.** Dwayne was a very good and smart man, but he couldn't sell his way out of a paper bag. He was afraid of his own shadow. <u>He was afraid of rejection</u>. Well, by then I'd already been selling for a couple years, and I'd already had 10,000 phones hung up on me, and doors slammed in my face, I was immune to it all. But some people, like Dwayne, just can't handle that. <u>They're not very aggressive and they don't have it within them to be turned down repeatedly</u>. Dwayne had had the money, and he had invested in this franchise, and his carpet cleaning van was just collecting dust because he didn't know how to go out there and hustle.

That's one man. Then there's my friend, Gary, from Brooklyn. Gary was a hustler. Now, he wasn't a real criminal; he was a good man, or he would have never been my best friend, I can promise you that. **But he was a hustler; he was a guy who just made things happen.** So even though we were broke and he was just out of prison, he wanted it so bad that we went ahead and started the business. **There were a million reasons why we shouldn't have done it; any rational person would have said, "No way," and in fact I had people who cared about me beg me not to do it, telling me I was crazy.** Other people laughed at me. They all said I was being swayed by Gary. We did it anyway, and the truth is, the partnership didn't last very long. We made it less than a year before it broke down. But by that time we had two carpet cleaning trucks and two sets of equipment, and our split was easy – we just cut the business in half, and he went his way and I went mine. We weren't friends anymore, unfortunately. **Business can complicate pre-existing relationships, so be careful about that.**

But the bottom line is: it didn't matter if we were broke. It didn't matter if we didn't have equipment. He went out and found a guy with this beat-up van he wanted $300 for. Well, we didn't have $300! So what did Gary do? He offers the guy a thousand bucks – a hundred dollars a week for 10 weeks. And if we missed even one payment during those 10 weeks, the guy got to keep all the money and we had to give him the van back. That was Gary.

Then he went out there and he found a little janitorial supply house in Wichita, and he hustled the guy and worked out a deal where we got all of our equipment without any money down. **Then he went out there and drummed up the business, just like I'd been drumming up the business.**

Even though it was the middle of winter and nobody wanted their carpets cleaned, we made it work. We got into these senior citizen towers over in Newton (there's two of them) and we just started knocking on doors and cleaning carpets and furniture. **We did great work, and they told their friends about us, and they told their friends.** We spent the winter of 1985-1986 working like crazy. We did almost every single apartment in these two senior citizen towers because we sat down with those older people, we ate food with them, we met them, we befriended them, we loved them, and they loved us. **We ended up surviving that difficult period because we treated our customers well, and we then built on those relationships.**

Even though our partnership ultimately folded, it was still a great partnership. I never would have gotten into business if it hadn't been for Gary. **We both had the right entrepreneurial skills, what I call "the skills of a salesperson," a hustler, somebody who's going to go out there and make it no matter what.** If you lack that, you need to find a partner who has it. The partnership may not last, but at least it'll get you started. That experience eventually led to me meeting my wife and forging a partnership that ended up making us millions of dollars. **When you get it right, success is a little like dominoes**: when one goes down, the next one falls, and the next one, and so on. But like Theodore Roosevelt once said, you have to, "Begin where you are with what you have."

I think if there's anyone who represents what a ruthless marketer is all about, it's Gary, who could sell to anyone and wouldn't take no for an answer. Now, Gary's a very flawed individual. He's a good person – he was raised right, and came from a good, solid family environment – but he's a little bit crazy, which I think is typical of all entrepreneurs. Compare him to Dwayne, another great guy, who was born with a silver spoon in his mouth, and lived in one of the nicest homes in the area. Dwayne had always had money; his life was always pretty much set. And yet, he got involved in this business and didn't know what to do with it.

I'm very proud to be an entrepreneur, and I love other people who share those types of dreams, who want to make things happen. Take my current best friend, who owns Midwest

Pest Control in Wichita, Kansas. Although Wichita's a relatively small market, she has over a hundred competitors – yet her company is one of the biggest and most successful in the business. Kerry Thomas, the guy who runs the whole thing for her, has this great quote that I just love because it's a ruthless marketing-type quote. Kerry once told me, **"Look, T.J., you're right. We do have a hundred competitors – but we have no competition."** I wrote that down in my journal that night, and I've been thinking about it ever since. Kerry's just made that way: he's got that swagger, that confident thing going, and his attitude has permeated the entire organization. All their pest control operators carry themselves confidently, their trucks are immaculately clean, their uniforms are crisply pressed, and their attitude is, "We're the best." As a matter of fact, that's part of their slogan: "If you want the best, call Midwest!"

Part of what the ruthless mindset is all about is having that attitude. It's a certain spirit, a way of believing, that can help you succeed no matter the obstacles. Gary had it, Dwayne didn't.

CHAPTER THREE

"Get the Proper Education"

As that clever old artillery captain, Harry S. Truman, once pointed out: "The 'C' students run the world." **My belief is that, for most intents and purposes, formal education is practically worthless in the real world**. For example, my friend John Alanis has a degree from the University of Texas in electrical engineering, and he tells me he still has trouble programming his DVR!

The problem is, theory and practice so often just don't meet. Here's a very revealing story about the "C" student from John's perspective. He and his classmates had a senior-level lab where they were supposed to implement the stuff they'd learned in theory – which is kind of like solving crossword puzzles and then making what you've learned work in the real world. In this kind of lab, you get all these electrical parts and try and put them together and make something work – and in John's lab, nothing they built would ever work.

You could take those gizmos to the professors, and they didn't have a clue why, despite the fact that they were supposed to be the experts. **The guys that get your gizmos to work are the techs**. They might not have a college education, but they know how to make the electronics work! They'll look at the parts and say something like, "Oh, well, the reason these things don't work is because those idiot students blew out the transformers." *Their minds weren't clouded by formal education*.

In most parts of the country, any publically-supported

school is really two separate schools. There's the general population of predominantly "C" students, and then you have Honors and Gifted classes where the students get a top-notch education. But you know what? **In politics and in society you don't really see those types of divisions**. I don't want to knock education, but the truth of the matter is <u>if you want to be a successful entrepreneur, there's no place you can go to school to learn it</u>. As it turns out, most entrepreneurs and other successful, self-made people are "C" students because they figured out early on that **what's taught in universities is pretty much irrelevant.**

It's that way even in public school. Chris Hollinger used to teach American Government, but what he taught was the way it was supposed to be – not how it really is, how it really works, with all the back-scratching and behind-the-scenes deals and corruption. Some students look at the world and very quickly recognize that what's being taught in school is pretty much worthless in the real world. You have to get outside the formal education system to find the stuff that really works.

Why is there such a market for John Alanis' products about dating and relationships? It's because the woman you're going to wind up marrying is a hugely important part of your life. **Make the wrong decision, and you're going to have a lot of problems financially, emotionally, and otherwise**. So John offers a system that can teach guys how to sift, sort, find, qualify, attract, and keep the right woman for them. Why is it so popular? Because there's no course taught in any school about that, even though maybe there should be – even if there aren't that many people qualified to teach it.

Look at college professors teaching management, business, or marketing. They're making a decent salary – maybe $50,000 or $60,000 a year – but many entrepreneurs who've never taken a single college course much more than that. At M.O.R.E., Inc., we've been known to make well over $100,000 in one day. Sure, that was gross income, but I think it illustrates a point: **if they're such experts, why aren't they making more money?** It's almost mind-boggling that they can make the kinds of claims they do.

The "C" student soon recognizes that formal education generally doesn't lead to practical education in the real world, and begins to turn his pursuits elsewhere – and so his grades suffer. In a way, many of these people are actually the "A" students: the go-getters and the technicians who know how the electronic components fit together. **These are the people who make things work in the real world because they have a thirst for practical education that's only graded by the results they get.** My recommendation is to seek out practical education from the people who are getting results, who are doing what they're saying, and <u>who are willing to teach other people to get results by doing what they're saying</u>.

There can be a big difference between theory and application – in fact, there usually is. **It's easy to theorize that something should work if it's done this way or that, but the theory is meaningless if you don't actually test it.** If you take an advertising class and come up with these big, pretty ads with lots of white space that are perfectly balanced, sure, that's going to get you an "A" in class. But go run one of those in the real world, where you have to write the check, and it has to work or you're suddenly deep in a financial hole – whew, it's a different deal! **It only takes one big chunk of money going away forever to figure out what works in the real world**. That's what separates the teachers from the doers: when you have to write that check to put that theory you're teaching into practice.

I've never been to college myself. But one of the people with which I work closely, Chris Lakey, has; he went to college for a year and hated it. Now, I realize that there are certain vocations where you must have a college education in order to work in the field. If you want to be doctor or a lawyer, there are certain things you have to do to get that piece of paper that says you've completed a certain amount of education. **But I think for most people, college just ends up being a waste of time.** I know people who are in their thirties and are still paying off college debt – and half of them aren't doing anything related to what they studied in college! So what good did that do them in the end? Maybe they've got a little bit more head smarts, <u>but that doesn't necessarily translate to practical sense</u>. When it comes down to it, it's the "A" and the "B" students who end up being teachers – which is perfectly fine. As they say, "Those who can, do. Those who can't, teach."

When it comes to education, you're typically going to get out of it what you put into it. **Education – especially higher education – is big business in this country, and people get paid by putting butts in the seats and tuition checks in the bank accounts**. So there's often a disconnect between what you've learned and the application of that knowledge, especially if you get a liberal arts degree – because where are you going to apply that? You don't get any real, concrete training when you receive a liberal arts degree, though in many ways, that degree does open up doors that otherwise aren't open in our society. **Now, what's happened is that some "C" students who saw that those doors were closed to them said, "Well, horse crap! I'm going through the door anyway – or <u>I'll make my own door.</u>"**

So get away from that whole institutionalized way thinking that says college is absolutely necessary for success. **Education can be helpful, there's nothing wrong with it for its own sake, and in many cases it can open a lot of doors for you. But, anyone who tells you you'll never get anywhere without it <u>doesn't know what they're talking about</u>**. That's not true, and plenty of people have proved it. They saw that in politics or in certain realms of our society, they were shut out because they didn't have a ring on their finger that said they were from a certain academy or college. **So, they created their own rules,** and we pay attention to that <u>because now they're super-successful</u>.

The truth about marketing and advertising as it's traditionally taught in colleges is that they don't teach you squat about the real world; they teach you theories out of textbooks, and that's it. **Realistic, practical training needs to be brought into the curriculum; for example, straightforward financial education**. They should also throw in some real-world applications of non-traditional enterprises – for example, how to make money from home, and how to be an entrepreneur. This is starting to happen now. For the first time, you're seeing this attitude reflected in some of the courses provided by a few progressive-thinking colleges and universities across the country. Wichita State, here in Kansas, has an entire entrepreneurial program. Some of the stuff I'm teaching you in this book should be in their curriculum…but I know it's not. They still teach a lot of cookie-cutter stuff, though part of the curriculum involves reading some of the books I'll be sharing with you in this book.

So some of it's getting there, and that's good. Soon you'll have kids coming out of colleges who don't want to go that traditional route of going to a big company and getting a job. **They're going to some of these entrepreneurial colleges just for that reason: so that they can get a foundation in marketing principals and go out there and apply them themselves, <u>on their own terms.</u>** But there's still going to be a big learning curve when they get out in the real world and realize how things truly work – **because there's always a big gap between what you learn and its application**.

Formal education has its place, and it offers certain advantages that can help make you a better person. I just happen to believe that, in almost every case, what they teach in business has no place in the real business world, unless of course you want to become a cog in a big corporate machine – and it probably won't even hold you in very good stead there. If you're an entrepreneur, forget it. However, college can effectively broaden your horizons. It can introduce you to new people and new types of people, and to whole new cultures and ideas that you might never have encountered before. And you don't have to matriculate at a fancy Ivy League school to get the benefit; state colleges are just fine. **In many ways, the experience of going to college, of making friends and learning to be an adult and competing with life, is wonderfu**l. For many of us, it broadens our depth of understanding of how things work, which gets internalized and comes out in whatever we do, including the ways we run our businesses.

But I want to emphasize again that you don't have to go to college to learn all that. You can teach yourself all the things you need to know, and broaden your own horizons, if you work hard and keep your eyes open. Don't let anyone tell you that you're shutting the door on your life if you don't get a college degree; if they do, give them the example of Bill Gates, the richest man in the world. He never finished college. He decided to get rich instead. If you're going to go to work as an employee for the rest of your life, sure, college does serve you well; some of my best staff members, including my current General Manager, are college-educated people. **Here's my take on why so many businesses really think a college education is important: not having one usually shows a lack of stability.** Somebody who's gone through four years of college is more stable, generally, than somebody who hasn't.

When I look at all the great entrepreneurs – when I think of those people who are reckless, who are rebellious, who are renegades – I'm so grateful that I grew up before they started feeding prescription drugs to hyperactive kids. In today's world they would have watched me, diagnosed me with Attention

Deficit Disorder, and drugged me to the gills. I couldn't sit still in class. I was bored to death. Drugs tame that spirit, and, in a way, so does college. I've got a good friend who's a Mensa member. You have to have a very high IQ to belong to Mensa, something like 140 or so, significantly higher than the average. This man should be an entrepreneur. He's got all the right qualities: he's independent, he's stubborn, he's rebellious, he likes to do everything his way, he's smart…and yet he tells me time and time again, "T.J., I know too many things that can go wrong." **That's what his education has done for him!** It's shown examples of all the things that can go wrong, and he just can't get them out of his head.

But I was a "C" student. I was young and dumb and didn't know any of those things. I jumped into business blindly with both feet, and I made mistakes along the way. I fell flat on my face, I picked myself back up, and I found people who are smarter than me with which to align myself – all because I didn't have that restless spirit medicated or educated out of me. I feel that, at some point, **formal education soon stops serving you and becomes a hindrance to success.** The less-educated people who have the willingness to go out there and screw up and pave their own path do tend to have some advantages.

Let me point out here that I'm talking about formal education; there are other types of education, and they're just as valuable, if not more so. **You shouldn't necessarily mistake a "C" student for somebody who's uninterested in education, especially if they've got that restless entrepreneurial spirit.** The reason they're "C" students (in the sense of formal education, anyway) is they just decided to seek education elsewhere. But they did still seek practical education, as opposed to all those guys who decided it was better to sit in a classroom and listen to a professor chatter away. **Practical business education wins hands-down over theory, every time**.

Here's an amusing point one of my seminar attendees, Everett, once made. A friend told Everett that he had an idea he was going to put into effect, making it into a business. Everett said, "You can't do that. You don't know anything about that." His friend replied, **"I don't have to. I can hire enough unemployed college professors to do whatever I want done."** And he's exactly right! I have direct experience with the same thing. When I was 16 years old and dropped out of high school for the first time, I worked on a landscape crew with four or five other guys. One of them had a Masters Degree. I later learned that he was making a whole dollar more per hour than I was – despite that advanced degree.

A Note About the Different Ways of Learning and Achieving

I find that most "C" students are hands-on people rather than intellectuals. They're often mechanically-inclined, people who are always doing things with their hands – which is why they're entrepreneurs. Bill Gates is that kind of person, or at least he was in the early days of his career. **There are all kinds of different learning styles, and there are different ways to rate intelligence besides the standard IQ tests.** That's one of the things you're probably going to start seeing more in our public education system soon – modalities or styles of teaching that address people who, like Chris Lakey, may be more logical, sequential learners, as opposed to people like me, who learn by doing and moving. Other people learn better by listening.

In my opinion, the "C" students who end up ruling the world are the types of people who realize early on that school probably isn't going to be for them, and so they're going to have to pave their own road – and sometimes have to hack that road out of a jungle with a machete. On the other hand, formally-educated people make the best employees to run their companies, so there's room for everyone – for all styles of learning – out there in the business world. **But, look closely at who's really earning the money and pulling the strings, and you'll see a lot of "C" students in the background.**

CHAPTER FOUR

Realize that "The Secret" is Really Hard Work

Most books on business success don't talk about the hard, focused work, the discipline, the sacrifice, and the commitments that characterize all super-successful people. Why? **Because this is not something that most people want to hear.** My best example is the popular book called *The Secret.* Like so many other books out there, *The Secret* tells you that everything will work out fine if you just think positively. That's all there is to *The Secret.* **If you believe in *The Secret*, God bless you – maybe there's some truth to it.** But it sounds like your basic wish fulfillment fantasy to me.

Books full of affirmation and similar New Age claptrap tend to sell a lot; people eat that stuff up. Hey, I do too! I'm not going to be a hypocrite and tell you I haven't spent a lot of money buying into the "three steps to this," "two steps to that," "one step to the other," "the one-minute whatever," or "the instant millionaire." But the bald truth is that while some of this stuff is helpful, most of it's crap.

Probably the best book on business I've ever read is called *McDonald's: Behind the Arches* by John F. Love; I mentioned it back in Chapter 1. It was written in the mid-1980s, so it's outdated a little, but I tell everyone about it. **Why they're not teaching this in business school is beyond me because this is the real, unvarnished truth about one man and his dream**, and what it took to create what's now the world's largest holder of commercial real estate in the world: the McDonald's Corporation. They're really in the real estate business, by the way, even though everybody thinks they're in the fast food business. And there's another book I just finished reading for the third time: it's called *Hard Drive*, and it tells the story of Microsoft. I've got other books about Microsoft, too, and I've got books about Steve Jobs, Michael Dell, and Sam Walton. **You read those books and you'll realize that the real formula for success is hard, focused work.** That's probably why they don't teach them in business schools: because that's not what people want to hear.

The willingness to put in hard, focused work is the common element in all the successful companies and entrepreneurs out there, and you'll see it repeated over and over in all personal and company biographies.

Look at people like Ray Kroc, who started with very little at the age of 52, and all the things it took to build McDonald's, a tremendous corporation that's still thriving years after his death.

Look at Bill Gates. The day he officially dropped out of college and told his father, "I'm not going back, Dad," his father said, "Son, you've just thrown your whole life away." Of course, we all know the story didn't turn out that way; he worked his tail off, and now he's reaping the profits.

When you read books about people who have actually turned small sums of money into huge fortunes, you'll find out they didn't use *The Secret* to make themselves the successes they are today. They didn't just sit around and affirm it all, and chant positive things, and get their minds right. All that has its place – attitude definitely plays a big role in success, there's no question about that – but it's hardly the major component in business success. **These people all worked hard, focused constantly on what they wanted, and practiced dramatic self-discipline and**

sacrifice to get where they are today.

So look at the facts, and let those facts guide you. Read the stories of other super-successful people, the ones that are mostly told in biographies (not autobiographies – they're too unreliable), and you'll find that it took a lot of work for that success to happen. They serve as models for all of us.

Let's look at Bill Gates again. **Want to talk about ruthless marketing?** Here is your primary model. He's one of the most ruthless marketers in history. Books like *Hard Drive* prove just how ruthless, how relentless, he is. When he got the IBM deal in 1981 – the catalyst for building his whole corporation – he called his Mom up. He used to go to his parents' house for dinner every Sunday, but after the IBM deal he told his mother, "Mom, I'm not going to see you or call you for the next six months. You're not going to hear from me." **He was so focused, so dedicated, so committed, so passionate about putting that whole thing together that he knew he was going to be sacrificing most of his personal life for a long time.** Whole weeks would go by, and he would barely leave his office. Sometimes he didn't even take time off to take a shower!

Another book of which I'm a big fan is Robert Ringer's *Winning Through Intimidation*. In that book, Ringer presents a view of business reality that I've found really holds up. **When a lot of people get into the business, they've got this idea that maybe they'll do a little bit of work, they'll become successful, and they'll stay that way.** In other words, they don't have a firm grasp of reality – and therefore, they make bad decisions about their business. **Let me reiterate this: the reality of succeeding in business, no matter the field, is to accept that you're going to have to devote a lot of time, energy, and effort to it if you want to succeed.** So you might as well recognize that and embrace it. Once you do, it turns you into a completely different person – and you realize that books like *The Secret* and

The Four Hour Work Week are so much B.S.. That's not to say that they're completely useless; there are some good ideas here and there, and they've got excellent marketing titles. But come on – affirming your way to success without working hard? Succeeding on four hours a week? **A lot of people want to accept the impression that they're going to be able to work four hours a week and spend the rest of the week screwing off, and they're still going to have a successful business.** If you believe that, well, I have this bridge in Brooklyn I can sell ya, cheap! Come on, you know none of that's true; if wishes were horses, beggars really would ride. <u>If you're going to run a successful business – if you're going to make money and keep your money – you'd better spend more than four hours a week working on it.</u>

The point is that if you want to be successful, you do have to devote a lot of time, energy, and effort to what you've chosen. But the other side of that coin is that it has to be something that you really believe is worth doing. There's a point where you have to look at what you're doing and say, "Look, if I don't want to devote everything I need to to this business, then I should quit trying to become successful from a financial point of view, and go off and just have a good time and do something else." <u>Because that's the price that has to be paid for success in any business. That's reality.</u> That's the real secret: you've got to recognize and embrace reality. That doesn't mean you can't enjoy yourself; applying the analogy of business as a game, you can find that playing this game really is a lot of fun. If you get into it, and it's the right thing, what you thought was work really isn't work after all. So you end up devoting a lot of hours to it, and the payoff both in financial terms and in what you become and achieve is well worth the effort that's involved. But, there is effort involved.

For years I've been accused of being a workaholic because I put in a lot of hours every week. But the truth is, a lot of what I do is anything but work. That's not to say that it's easy; that's not to say that I'm not putting in a lot of effort. But it's fun, so putting in long hours doesn't burn me out. I think for a lot of business people, "work" is a nasty four-letter word. The way that they look at their businesses causes working in them to be real drudgery. Whereas to an entrepreneur, work is fun – it's interesting, it's challenging. **You put your passion into it, your excitement, your enthusiasm, and it actually enhances rather than depletes you. It actually builds you up**.

Chris Hollinger told me a story recently about going into a convenience store to get some Gatorade after a stiff game of basketball with his brother. He found a little newspaper called *The Rural Messenger* that included a quote from Henry David Thoreau that went something like this: ***"The cost of anything is measured in the amount of life you're willing to exchange for it."*** After Chris read it aloud, the lady who was working behind the counter looked at him and said, "What am I doing here?" She was trading those hours that she spent behind the counter for a paycheck at the end of the week. **And Chris got to reflecting about how, given the astronomical number of hours he and his wife were putting into their business, they ought to be total wiped out by the end of the week.** If they'd been putting in that time in a classroom or regular job they sure would have been. But they're not! They're energetic and happy with their work.

Here's a good way to make you understand that: look at a time in your life when you were doing something you were good at, and you really had fun doing it…like a hobby or vocation. **It can even be something hard, like algebra, once that light bulb clicks on in your head – suddenly it makes sense, everything works, and you look forward to doing it.** It's not work. <u>That's how it is with direct-response marketing</u>, once you get in the groove. It's a lot of work putting the systems together, getting the back-end offers all ready, building the lead generation systems, and then building that relationship with customers. Sure, it can be a lot of work. But man, it's a great game to play!

The Real Power of a Positive Attitude

Real success requires a lot of real work – enjoyable work, maybe, but hard work nonetheless. Nothing's just going to come to you unless you're incredibly lucky. But should you throw *The Secret* out the window altogether? Actually, no. The book has a few ideas that are worth listening to. **The most important thing you can learn from it is that an optimistic and positive attitude, is self-fulfilling. Whereas if you think negatively of yourself all the time, you may never take that first step that leads you to the answer you need.** The danger is that some of these books on manifestation and affirmation take advantage of people by making them believe that as long as they think those positive thoughts, everything will come to them automatically. My mentor Dan Kennedy has a real good take on that. He says that all that stuff is fine, but it's a lie of omission, because in addition to having a positive attitude, you have to have a realistic attitude toward work. **They tell you, "If you just do it you'll get the results," but don't mention that you have to take action in conjunction with that positive attitude**.

And I understand that. It's based on an important marketing principle: **sell people what they want, give them what they need.** I could write a sales letter right now that said, "Look, I've got this great business opportunity; it's got the potential to make you a lot of money, but you're going to have to work long hours. You're going to have to bust your butt. You're going to have to put in the time," and guess what? There's no way that I would make any sales.

Frankly, I probably wouldn't be here today if that hadn't happened to me. If people would have told me how difficult some things that I've gone after really would be, and the price that I'd have to pay to achieve some of the things I've achieved in this world, there's no way I would have ever gotten started. I promise you that. **Back in the 1980s, I just wanted to become a millionaire; I didn't want to have to do all the things I've had to do to develop my knowledge and skills and whatever abilities I've managed to acquire so far**. Other people are the same way, and they've helped us build our business. We've got programs where we do everything for the customer. And yet the people who want to make the most money are the ones who take it way beyond all that.

Case in point: the first distributorship we made available was called "Dialing For Dollars." We sold 150,000, and out of those we had maybe five or six hundred people who were really successful. Think about that. That's kind of shocking to some people, but not to those who understand how it worked. When we were just a baby company back in 1989 or 1990, one guy was doing $5 million a year working our "Dialing For Dollars" program, when we were only doing about two million a year. **He was doing more than twice the amount of business we were doing, and he was one of our distributors!** But he was a renegade in every way. **He broke all the rules we outlined in our "Dialing For Dollars" book – everything we told him to do, he did the exact opposite and he was making the most money out of all of them!** He tested a lot of things. He tried a lot of things. He had his own ideas. He was independent. He was a ruthless marketer!

Remember what Henry David Thoreau said: *"The cost of anything is measured by the amount of life you're willing to exchange for it."* If you want to make millions of dollars, there's no easy simple way to do it that I know of. And I would be very suspicious of anybody who came along and told me that there was. In fact, I'd grab my wallet and start backing away toward the door! That was my point in discussing the business biographies earlier. These are the people who have paid the largest price in terms of the sacrifice, the commitment, the dedication, the hours they've put into their enterprises. Those entrepreneurs are people who are willing to do for a short time what most people are not willing to do at all.

Take the example of Bill Gates, when he was just absolutely focused for six months. Sure, he went to the Mercedes dealer and got a new Mercedes. But the first thing he told them before he drove it off the lot was, "I want you to take the radio out of it." When they asked, "Why?" He just said, "Just do it." **The reason he took his radio out of the car was, he didn't want any distractions**. While he was driving to and from work, he just wanted to stay focused on his work. That's an extreme example, but still it represents a man who was totally into his vision. He didn't want anything to get in the way of his thinking through where he was headed. **If you really want to make a lot of money, you'll have to be that focused on your business, too**. As Abraham Lincoln once put it, *"Good things come to those who wait, but only what's left over from those who hustle."*

CHAPTER FIVE

"Be Audacious!"

Entrepreneurs are audacious. We are bold, daring, risk-takers. We live to play the game.

I like to tell the story of Jerry Wilson, the entrepreneur behind Soloflex and Bowflex. He used to be a charter jet pilot, and his job was flying high-rollers into Las Vegas. After observing and interacting with wealthy passengers for years, he came to realize that <u>none of them was any smarter than he was</u>. **But they had something in common: audacity, which just means that they were willing to stick it all out there on the line.**

When you compare entrepreneurs with people who just live their 9-to-5 job every day until they retire, you'll find that's what separates them is that: entrepreneurs are risk-takers. They step out on a limb. They don't take standing still well. **They always have to be moving forward. They always have to be trying the next big thing**. They're always looking for another adventure. They're always looking for the next item they're going to test, the next product they're going to invest in, another revenue stream. Sure, a lot of them go through ups and downs in life. They have moments where they're on top of the hill, and they've got a product or a business that's working really well. But you'll also find them at the bottom of the valley sometimes, after they've hit rock bottom, they've had a business fail and things aren't going well.

Yet they continue to take risks.

A few years back, there was an entrepreneur who decided that Wichita needed a theme park, and he bet $30 million that he could make it work. The only problem was, he thought it was only going to take $15 million when he got started, so he outran his capital and ended up going bankrupt, and the park is up for sale now. They're hoping they find a buyer before they liquidate all the rides and they all go back to their vendors. The park opened in May, and by the end of the summer it was out of money, and had to close. Costs were about twice what the founder thought they were going to be. **But he had an existing business that was very profitable, and served the marketplace well**. It was a show and dinner theatre. Every night, people came to his ranch and got a country/western show and dinner, and he was wildly successful. Business was growing, expanding, and doing extremely well.

Then he had this vision to build an amusement park, and he spent all his savings on it. He got all kinds of people to invest money in this dream, about which he was extremely confident – but when it cost twice what he expected, that was it. He ended up going bankrupt. He even lost the successful business, because he spent a lot of that capital to get the new business going; recently they auctioned it off, and he lost virtually everything. He actually had to move out of state because of all the negativity surrounding him and his story. **He's going to try to start anew somewhere else. But I can guarantee you: this isn't his last business.** Yes, he's at the bottom of the ladder right now; he's as low as you can get on the success vs. failure scale. I don't know him personally, but I'm sure that because he's the kind of an entrepreneur that he is, he'll soon be running a new business somewhere. **He'll find a way to be successful because that's just the way entrepreneurs are.**

You know, a lot of people in business have people telling them they don't know what they're doing, that they shouldn't be in business. But successful entrepreneurs ignore the advice of their peers. They ignore all the people who tell them why their business shouldn't work. There's something to be said about entrepreneurs who start young because, usually, as you get older, you start getting more set in your ways. You tend to take fewer risks as you get older. **And yet, in any stage of life it's all about deciding that you're going to jump in, and that you're going to go for it. And, you've got to be audacious.**

It's a good thing just to remember that entrepreneurs take risks. We're a unique breed because most people don't have the audacity – the guts – to take those kinds of risks required to succeed in business. I think it goes back to that entrepreneurial mindset that you absolutely have to depend on because there will be a lot of people out there who will try to talk you down.

Take my colleague, Chris Hollinger, who used to be a schoolteacher. When he told his colleagues that he was stepping out of the classroom, where he'd been for ten years, they said, "What are you going to do? How are you going to make it?" They thought he was crazy. And maybe he is, a little bit! **Maybe you have to be crazy to be audacious enough to succeed at business**.

Here's another thing about Chris Hollinger, an inspirational story if there ever was one: he's a cancer survivor. It wasn't until shortly after he survived a deadly bout with cancer that he decided to become self-employed, and I'm sure that some of the people cautioning him thought those two items were related. And maybe it was a wake-up call for him and his entrepreneurial dreams because when he went back to work, he had visions of small businesses and things that he could try.

Yes, he was tempted to stay a teacher, due to the lure of that steady paycheck and the fact that he's got relatives and in-laws who are all teachers. I know his wife really liked the idea of a steady paycheck, too. But when the sales started rolling in, she got hooked! **Being your own boss, marketing your own products, is a very addictive lifestyle**. I can tell you right now that Chris is utterly ruined as an employee, just like me Russ Von Hoelscher, John Alanis, and most of my friends who are marketers. After this kind of lifestyle, there's absolutely no way any of us could go back to being anybody's employee. We'd be miserable, and we'd make everyone around us that way, too. **It's that mindset that really carries you through some of the ups and downs that this business can have. Develop it, nurture it, and relish it because it's all part of the lifestyle.**

Most people outside our business just don't get it. There's a kind of stigma attached to wealthy entrepreneurs – in the sense that people think that somehow those people are special, or they know more than everyone else does, or whatever. **But that's all nonsense.** That's the secret Jerry Wilson learned, back before he started Soloflex. Here's a man who was making a good six-figure income flying high rollers back and forth from L.A. to Vegas. He knew flight so well that he'd put it on automatic pilot for 30 or 45 minutes, and he'd go back and talk to his wealthy guests. And he got to know them well over a period of time, just because he kept flying the same multi-millionaires and billionaires back and forth.

So he was getting to be about 50 years old and one morning, as the story goes, while he was shaving, it suddenly dawned on him that the only real difference between him and those high-rollers he'd been flying was that they had this audacity that came out in everything they did. Shortly after that he quit his job, started Soloflex…and we all know the rest of that story.

I think that entrepreneurs tend to see things differently than most business owners do. **Entrepreneurs see business more as a game; they don't even think like traditional business owners**. To them, they're in it for the passion, the joy, the sport of it all. Whereas, I think most business owners look at it more as a job, or as an excuse to do something and not have their own boss. They're very myopic in their vision. **Most business owners work in their business, not on their business**, because they think the business is the doing of the thing; whereas the entrepreneur sees that the business is the marketing, the building of systems, the moving off of those systems to other people, and that it's all about growth.

Careful Audacity is Not a Contradiction in Terms

I think a lot of people who want to run their own businesses and be successful get sidetracked because they get to a point where they're going to have to spend a little money or take a little risk, and they become fearful. That fear stops them in their tracks. **The entrepreneurial trait that overcomes that is audacity – the ability to get past that and take the actions necessary**. Audacity is really just another way of saying that entrepreneurs take action, even when – especially when – the going gets tough. A lot of people won't take action because they have a lot of questions in their minds. They want to get all their questions answered before they do something; they want to find the experts before they even get started. I've seen these people at seminars: they've been going to seminars for twelve years, and they've never done anything. What they don't understand is that answers come from action. **No entrepreneur out there has all the answers, and there's no way you can know the answers until you take action on a particular product.** Now, you may get good answers, you may get bad answers…but you get answers, and it directs you where you need to go. And so audacity leads to answers, which lead to action.

A key skill you absolutely have to develop along with audacity is measured risk-taking: the ability to look at a

particular project or business and make realistic real-world decisions about how it will work out or flop. If it fails, what are the consequences? If it succeeds, where are you going to go from there? That's measured risk-taking – not taking a spray-and-pray approach or falling in love with a bright, shiny object that looks really good. It's developing the skill of taking measured risks and then, once you've measured the risks, taking action, knowing that answers lie on the other side of that coin. This action-taking is a key entrepreneurial trait, but remember this: those actions always have to be calculated.

While you want to be audacious and want to be bold and take risks, you want to take measured risks. Too many people out there take stupid risks – like all those people who invested blindly in those dot-com companies back before the year 2000. Taking stupid risks is a good way to go broke and stay that way. You know how I know that? Because I've taken stupid risks in the past, and I've lost millions. On the other hand, I've also taken carefully thought out, calculated risks, and I've made millions more.

The point is, answers come from action. If you're confused about something, take action. You'll get some answers. They may not be the ones you want, but you'll get them, and they'll lead you to the ones that you do want. In many ways, it's more of a game than anything else. It's a challenge. Those of us who are sports fans know that losing is all part of the game. In our market you can test very aggressively; you can do all kinds of outrageous, wild, expensive kinds of things. But that's okay, as long as you're testing it in small numbers; you might lose a few thousand, but you're not going to lose hundreds of thousands or even millions.

On the other hand, if you're audacious enough and it works, you've got a veritable gold mine on your hands.

The Ruthless Marketing Attack!

CHAPTER SIX

"Be a Troublemaker"

Sometimes audacity isn't enough.

According to Harvard Business professor Abraham Zaleznik, "If you want to understand the entrepreneur, we should look at the juvenile delinquent."

Another professor, Mason Cooley, tells us, **"Entrepreneurship is the last refuge of the troublemaking individual."** And it's true. There's a certain energy or spirit that goes with all great entrepreneurs that's synonymous with many tendencies that juvenile delinquents have, in terms of rebelliousness, at least.

When you study the lives of people who are great entrepreneurs, you'll see that rebellious streak in all of them. It's especially true for younger entrepreneurs. I know it was part of my youth. I was rebellious. **I followed my own path, and refused to do what everybody told me I should do.** I see that in a lot of younger people today. For example, I've got a kid working in shipping who's dying to be an entrepreneur. He's cocky. He thinks he knows everything; he feels invincible. **He doesn't realize that he's mortal, and all that. But that's okay!** **That kind of attitude can serve you well in business**.

I've studied the lives of hundreds of people who've made millions or billions after starting out with nothing, and I can tell you that they've all got that renegade nature inside of them, the one you see in a lot of juvenile delinquents – where they're not going to take no for an answer, and nobody is going to tell them what to do. By God, they're going to do everything their way. Do those people go bankrupt a lot? Sure they do. Do they make bad mistakes? Absolutely. **But behind every great company – especially the ones that started up and made it big quickly – there's an entrepreneur who was rebellious, who was more of a renegade than anything else**. My best example is Bill Gates. He's notorious for being a big pain in the ass; the stories about him are legendary. Nobody could ever tell him anything; he argued with everybody.

You see, entrepreneurs create chaos. It's a necessary trait in the entrepreneur. That said, the entrepreneur who wants to be successful and stay that way has to build a team of people who can make up for all their weaknesses. They've got to find people who are stable, which a lot of entrepreneurs are not; they need a team to manage the chaos they create, made up of people who aren't afraid to tell them when they're about to screw up the whole company. They've got to find a good number-cruncher and others who can pay attention to details. In my case, I had two business partners before I met my wife. She became my third business partner, and was the only one that lasted. I don't want to minimize their roles in my career – after all, they helped me get started – but those relationships were very short-lived. **It wasn't until I found a partner who was my complete opposite that I became successful**.

Now, Eileen and I are alike enough to keep our marriage together and hang out together, but in every other way she's totally my opposite; she's so conservative, whereas I'm anything but. But that's good, because there has to be that balance in any business situation. Part of that balance is somebody who is radical, extremely ambitious, totally driven, and a little bit reckless at times; some people may call it "visionary," although that's an overused word. But they have to be offset by the quiet conservatives who can keep them sane and on the straight and narrow.

Delinquent Doesn't Mean Stupid

Back when he was a teacher, Chris Hollinger had the privilege of having some really sly, sneaky 15-year-old boys and girls sitting in his classroom who didn't want to be there. They didn't want to have anything to do with U.S. History, World Geography, or Government – and yet, the law said they had to attend. And invariably, he'd find himself drawn to these kids one way or another. I like to joke that it's because like attracts like, and there's some truth in that. **But the point is that like "ruthless," "delinquent" is another word that conjures up negative images – despite the fact that these kids are usually pretty smart**. Take Albert Einstein. He was considered delinquent in school, because he was sitting there bored in class all the time. But he came up with some of his best theories while he was off daydreaming. So there's a spark there – and orneriness has its own spark. **It has its own spirit, and can drive the soul and the entrepreneur to do great things.**

The Value of Non-Conformity

Here's another aspect that marks the successful entrepreneur, and it's associated as equally with the unwillingness to accept the traditional as it is with the willingness to work hard and focus on what matters, rather than what someone else thinks should matter. **The best, most successful entrepreneurs tend to be non-conformists.**

Think about what you're told practically from the moment you're born. You've got parents telling you, "Be careful! Watch out! No, don't touch that!"

From the time you're born, there's this sphere of protection buffering you from the world. This is good, obviously, but if it's overdone you grow up with this "be careful" mentality instead of an audacious "put it all out there and risk everything" mentality. That's the opposite of what culture tells you in the "be careful" mode. Even in school, all the way back to Kindergarten, you're taught to conform. <u>The last thing that a successful entrepreneur should do is conform</u>. You have to strike out and go your own way. **Sometimes, you're going to end up in the middle of nowhere, and sometimes you're going to make mistakes – and sometimes that action leads to the answer.**

In some situations, conformity is a good thing. But I think that after you learn to conform, then you've gotta learn to un-conform as a marketer, and know when to violate the rules and when to abide by them. You're going to find that almost every great entrepreneur is a non-conformist, **because conformity leads to conventional results**. If you work like that, you're going back to that "me too" attitude that stunts a lot of businesses. **Most businesses are doing exactly the same thing as all of their competitors; everybody is following the follower**. There's nothing unique. There's nothing that separates one from the other. Do you think Michael Dell got rich this way? How about Sam Walton, or Bill Gates? No, no, and hell no!

If you always do what people tell you, if you follow conventional wisdom, you're going to get conventional results. The success enjoyed by all the greatest companies and the greatest entrepreneurs has come out of unconventional things that have gone against the grain of what others recommended. These people and companies are doing their own thing. **Yes, a lot of them get in trouble; but like your average juvenile delinquent, they tend to be pretty resilient and bounce back quickly, and then they go off and create more trouble**. Like juvenile delinquents, they can't help themselves.

CHAPTER SEVEN

"Stay a Little Paranoid"

Some level of paranoia is an integral part of business success. Not clinical paranoia, the type that has you afraid to move because you think there's a bad guy behind every tree; I'm talking about the subtle sense that you have to stay on your toes, or someone out there's going to overtake you, and you're going to be left behind. Because in business, that's the way it is – <u>the harsh reality is that you have to stay a little worried, or suddenly you're yesterday's news.</u>

Successful entrepreneurs wake up every day a little paranoid that something bad is going to happen. It's just part of the life of the business owner. **There's such a thing as "healthy paranoia," because if you're not proactive about solving problems, bad things are likely to sneak up on you.** You need to continually ask yourself, "What's going to go wrong? How can I figure it out? How am I going to deal with things when they go wrong? How am I going to deal with it when this marketing campaign doesn't work as expected? How am I going to deal with it when the idiot ad rep puts the ad on the left-hand page instead of the right? How am I going to deal with it when the post office treats my pre-sorted, first class mailing as bulk?" When you're paranoid about all these things, it orients your mind towards solutions for the times when these things come up. **People who aren't paranoid in business panic when something goes wrong, because they're not anticipating problems.** Remember that old saying: "Just because you're paranoid doesn't mean they're not out to get you!"

You can go further than that and say, "I'm going to get them before they get me!" That's a pretty healthy attitude – and it's why my colleague John Alanis starts his work week on a Sunday night. He says he doesn't like Mondays, because he knows something bad is always going to happen on a Monday. So he makes his list on Sunday and decides, **"I'm going to get them on Monday before they get me,"** because like most entrepreneurs, he's preparing for the worst and he's paranoid that something bad is going to happen. Now, at the end of the day on Monday, usually nothing bad has happened; or anything that came up was minor and was dealt with easily, because John's been very proactive about this kind of thing.

Now in John's case, he got a lot of this mindset when he was a submariner in the Navy. You can bet healthy paranoia's a survival trait in that situation! He tells me that all they did there was drill. You model what can go wrong, and what's going to happen if it does go wrong. For example, "What happens when we only operate on half electrical power? What happens if a torpedo hits in this or that compartment? What can go wrong, and how can we anticipate it?" That was drilled into his head, and it turned out to be a very useful skill, **because he's always looking, anticipating, and thinking about what could go wrong**. That's why you should always pay your taxes on time. If we don't pay our taxes, we know what the I.R.S. is going to do to us.

The guys who aren't paranoid are the guys who get in trouble, because they go in with their eyes wide shut, with a song in their heart and not a care in the world, and they think nothing bad is going to happen. Then they have this dumb look on their face when the cops are hauling them away to jail, because they didn't think about all the things that could go wrong. So I'm a big believer in healthy paranoia. It's an entrepreneurial mindset that you need to have: **"I'm a paranoid ruthless marketer; that's what I am."**

The Ruthless Marketing Attack!

My company is in a market that's heavily regulated. There are all kinds of "regulatory police" watching our market. Everyone from the F.T.C. to the U. S. Postal Inspectors to any local government prosecutor can take shots at us. Unfortunately, the real criminals always stay about three steps ahead of the law and are really hard to catch, so the regulatory police who monitor our industry tend to come after easier targets, which are the ones sitting right there in the open, so they don't have to expend very much effort to do their jobs. **Take it from me, you've got to keep your nose as absolutely clean as possible, because Big Brother is watching!**

While fear is definitely an enemy to business success – in fact, too much of it can hold you back and keep you from following your dreams – a certain level of fear is healthy. It's an important survival skill. The best advice I ever received from my good friend, Alan R. Bechtold, was when we were discussing exactly this subject, and I was telling him about how concerned I was about what I see as the over-policing of our industry. Alan told me, "T.J., you don't have to worry about the F.T.C., postal inspectors, or any of those guys, if you'll always just pretend like they're watching every move that you're making. Every word that comes out of your mouth, every sentence you write on a sales letter, just pretend they're right there looking over your shoulder." So my paranoia comes from always being very careful about what I say – what I promise people, and what I don't promise people. **If you read our sales letters closely, you'll see that we put plenty of things in there just in case we ever have to defend ourselves.** That's really what being legal is all about.

Even better, in my way of thinking, the words defendable and legal are one and the same, because the law is so complicated, and it's always changing. My father was a lawyer, and when he graduated from law school you could pile all the laws in Kansas on a small table. But when he retired 35 or 40 years later, the legal code – just for this one state – was many

---

times bigger.

You see, they almost never go back and pull out laws that are no longer adequate, accurate, or applicable – they just pile on new laws. So the laws are very complicated nowadays, and frankly there's a lot of crap in there. It's hard to even walk down the street without breaking some law on the books somewhere. **At our company, we focus on defensibility as far as it's possible with our understanding of the law**. I'm very paranoid. I'm almost 50 years old now – the last thing I ever want to do is get in legal trouble.

Among other things, you need to be very careful when you hype your products, so you don't step over the line into what the law calls "puffery." There's an acceptable level of hype that's absolutely legal – as long as whatever you're promising you're willing to follow through on. What's not legal is this: when you promise somebody, "You will make this amount of money!" You have to be very careful about any income claims; there have to be disclaimers. **With a lot of marketers, the disclaimers are in the tiny, fine print at the bottom of their letters and ads.** We prefer to be more upfront about it and print our disclaimers in plain English that's easy to read and understand.

Besides over-hyping their services or products and then not following through, a lot of businesses get in trouble because they don't refund, especially in our market. In fact, if you'll look at the case histories, you'll see that just about everybody who's gone down in the Direct-Response Marketing business has gone down because they weren't refunding. Their customers complain and complain, and eventually it brings scrutiny from the regulatory bodies, and they say, "Hmm, these guys aren't refunding…these are bad guys. Let's go see what else we can get them for."

For the most part, if you're running a clean shop, you're refunding people when they request it, and you're maintaining good relationships with your customers – then you're going to be okay. So stay paranoid! Follow the most important rules! **The instant you start doing things like not giving people refunds and making outrageous, insane claims, you're going to get into trouble.** You can still be ruthless and follow the rules. Here's an example: I don't like making refunds, but I do make them. I even refund on products there's no refund on – that is, on products people bought without any guarantee or if the guarantee has expired. I don't like it, but I do it. But that has a consequence for the person I'm refunding to as well. **When someone demands too many refunds from me, I refuse to do business with them in the future.** I ban them for two reasons: 1) Because I don't like habitual refunders; and 2) I don't want to sell them something again, because I know they're going to demand a refund again. They're a problem customer and so by banning them, I'm getting rid of potential future problems.

CHAPTER EIGHT

"Be Willing to Grow"

One of the most important decisions you'll ever have to make – or series of decisions, really, since you'll probably face this issue repeatedly over the course of your business life – **is how and when to develop a business infrastructure**. It can be a tough decision, one that may ultimately be based on your personality and needs. Some of us find out that we need a lot more help than we anticipated and become "empire-builders," as my wife and I have been accused of being; but some of us design our businesses from the beginning to be single-person, employee-proof affairs.

John Alanis is a good example of the latter. When he started out, he set up a lot of his business on the Internet, using a web-based database and a lot of lead generation material that could be handled by automatic computer systems. He also contracted with good vendors who could perform all the other functions he needed: for example, he used a Kansas mailing house and printer for all his mailing, he had an independent vendor who did all his fulfillment for him, and he used an independent customer service company to handle all his customer service needs. **They pay for the infrastructure; he doesn't.**

He has someone he contracts to perform bookkeeping and media buying, and if he runs into something that he knows will start taking up a lot of his time, he'll contact one of the companies he works with and move that task to them. So all in all, he's pretty much been able to stay an independent operator. **He hasn't needed to make it any more complicated than he** wants it to be, and that's how he planned it from the beginning. As he puts it, "I don't want to be a zookeeper."

I'm at the opposite end of that spectrum. My company has an extensive infrastructure; I've surrounded myself with people who can do things I can't, and it works well for me. **So both schemas have their advantages and disadvantages**. I will say this: the whole time my wife ran the company – which she did for the first fourteen years – I always felt that I could do a better job than she did. I never really told her that, but I imagine she knew that's how I felt. **I thought I could a better job mainly because I was willing to work a lot more hours than she did and does. And I cared about the company so deeply, so passionately, that I just knew I could do a better job.** So when she stepped down in 2001 I had my chance! I came in and took over with that attitude that I was going to take on the world. But within a few years, I found out that, first of all, I'm the world's worst manager. Second, **it turned out that Eileen had been making it look easy all those years because she's got the natural skills of a great manager. She didn't have to bust her tail and put in 16-hour days to do the job right**.

So now I've got a good General Manager, Shelly. She has a lot of Eileen's qualities. She's a real common-sense type person, and she thinks pretty much like Eileen on a lot of issues. During those two or three years without a good General Manager, when I tried to run the business on my own, I was going home beat up every day. My hair started falling out, and it was just terrible. **At the time, I understood nothing about what some people call "energy management."** That's where you take the parts of your business that create a big energy drain for you and move them off to other people who are much better suited to deal with them. That's why I wanted Shelly to take the job of General Management off my plate. **In the end I had to put limits around myself so I could maintain my focus, so I could take my energy and devote it to the**

important parts of the business – writing the ads and sales letters, creating products, getting more customers through joint ventures, and similar functions. All the other issues were handed to other people who were much more qualified to deal with them than I was, who can better absorb all the energy drains that come with them.

What you should do, in regards to infrastructure, really depends on your vision and what you need. If you're looking for leadership, you want certain qualities like vision and direction; so you're looking for that delinquent who can really push people into doing things. In other situations, you may need someone with innate organizational skills and the power to be that good manager, like Eileen was for our business for all those years – she had that skill-set that allowed her to take care of many problems and say, "Okay, this is the way it's going to be." I know that my colleague Chris Hollinger has had a similar experience. He co-founded GoldMine Web Design and Marketing with his wife, Kim, and he tells me it wouldn't be half of what it is without her. She takes care of so many of those details, and that allows Chris to focus on other things that bring in a lot of money. If he were sitting there having to figure his taxes and deal with his accountant, he wouldn't get as much work done.

The Consequences of Trying to Do It All

The point here, is that unless you're some kind of superhuman, you can't do it all. Let me use a personal example. After my wife stepped down from running M.O.R.E., Inc., and before I learned how to hand off some of my tasks to people who could do them better, I was a basket case. Not only was I working myself sick, I almost ran my company into the ground. For a while there, I was a reverse millionaire: in other words, I owed over a million dollars more than my net worth.

Now, everybody wants to hear about the millions of dollars that we've made; nobody wants to hear about the millions of dollars we've lost. But our fortune has risen and fallen over time, and this is something you'll see a lot with other entrepreneurs. Bill Gates is an exception; he's rarely ever lost money. But Steve Jobs, the head of Apple Computers, has lost money. Ray Kroc, who made McDonald's a success, lost money on a number of different deals. **Sometimes losing is all part of winning – and you learn a lot in the end**.

What I learned is that you keep moving forward. You don't give up. You take your licks and grow stronger. Here's a quote from William A. Ward that sums it up: *"Adversity causes some men to break, others to break records."* I've experienced a lot of problems with my business, and they've all been my fault. They've almost all occurred when I haven't practiced one of the things that I preach in this book, which is that if you're going to test things, you test them in small increments. So if you lose, you only lose small amounts of money. I've done a lot of stupid things that have caused me to go deeply into debt. I've used aggressive marketing methods that have gotten me in trouble before because I've over-extended myself and leveraged myself out. I didn't follow my wife's lead; I didn't manage the company as she did for the first 14 years.

Eileen is such a conservative person, so careful, so cautious. For example, she always insisted that for every dollar we spent on advertising, we made it back immediately. And I always knew that the companies who were making huge sums of money in Direct Response Marketing weren't being so cautious. When it came to the marketing, Eileen used to say that her #1 rule at M.O.R.E., Inc., was, "We're never going to lose money on the front-end." And yet, I knew that this wasn't how those other companies thought of it. **They didn't think of it as "losing" money on the front-end; they looked at it as an investment towards future profits. <u>But, that's dangerous thinking when</u>**

The Ruthless Marketing Attack!

you extend it too far.

This is exactly what I did. At one point, the first time I became a reverse millionaire, **we had a promotion where initially we were spending $500, on average, to make every $50 sale.** It worked beautifully for a while, because we had a $2,500 up-sell and we had monthly continuity attached to it. And trust me, we were watching the numbers. The only problem is, the gap started stretching out from three to four months before we started making our initial costs back, then to five months…and then to six months…and then seven months…and then eight months! Even then, we were still making it work; we were still bringing in millions of dollars. In fact, that was the best year (so far) we've ever had for sales; we did almost $20 million that one year. But towards the end of the promotion, it got to be nine months before we were making our initial investment back. We were leveraged out. Even though we were having months where we were bringing in $2 million, our debt just kept growing and growing. Then the promotion died out, and I was left with a huge amount of debt and not enough cash flow...

That was the first time I became a reverse millionaire, and it was all through my own stupidity. **I was trying to emulate the big companies that use those tactics successfully.** But AHA! The difference is, when they get into heavy debt, all they have to do is say, "Well, let's sell a few hundred thousand shares of our stock, and that'll handle it. No big deal. We've got millions of shares to play with." But guess what? I didn't. M.O.R.E., Inc. isn't a publically traded company, and I didn't have those kinds of deep pockets to fall back on.

They say that whatever doesn't kill you makes you stronger, and failing that way did toughen me up. It wised me up, and taught me how to leverage my #1 strength. **Everybody reading this has something that's their #1 strength; it's up to you to figure out what that is.** But the thing to keep in mind is that <u>for most people, that #1 strength is also their #1 weakness</u>; I swear that's true. My #1 strength is the fact that I'm stubborn as hell. And yet, it's also one of my greatest weaknesses, because stubborn people don't listen to anybody. And so I have to learn the hard way. Every lesson that I've had to learn in my life has had a lot of pain attached to it, just because I'm stubborn and rebellious.

I've learned the hard way that you can't do it all. You need to look for people with which to work build a team and partner; folks who have skills that are complimentary to yours. That's what makes Eileen and I such a good team. Every company needs an entrepreneur, a juvenile delinquent who creates chaos because they can't help it, but they also need somebody to keep the house in order. That's because the skills that cause you to make a lot of money and the skills that are required for you to keep that money are usually very different. **In general, people who are really good at making money are really bad at keeping it.** I'm one of them, to a degree, because I've made some terrible mistakes. But I personally know people who are much worse than I am – brilliant marketers who can make millions of dollars but are always broke.

How can somebody who's so talented when it comes to making money be such a mess?

My observation is that the making of money and the keeping of money involve two separate and disparate skill sets that, at times, simply butt heads. That's because keeping money is a more conservative process than making it. You've got to take risks and be fiscally liberal to make money, but you have to be fiscally conservative to make it last. **If you're working a one-person operation, you've got to bridge the gap and have a very disciplined system where you take some of the money that's made and move it into a safe harbor where it's never touched.**

CHAPTER NINE

"Hope for the Best, Prepare for the Worst..."

Every business owner has their dream, or they wouldn't be in business. We all need to be audacious, to take calculated risks to get to where we want to go. We want to be ruthless, aggressive, go-getters. **But part of being properly ruthless is learning how to fail successfully.** If that sounds like an oxymoron, you don't have your head in the right place quite yet. **What I mean is this: you need to be able to prepare for the worst possible outcome, to set your company up so you can still make money with terrible numbers.** It's possible to do this realistically, in such a way that you can, by other people's definitions, fail – and still make money.

This is a very important point that you'll have to grasp before you can be truly successful in this field. **Some business owners never learn this.** I've met people who think they're going to succeed in Direct Response Marketing because they've got a $29.95 product that the whole world wants, and they're going to go out and sell it to them – and they have no chance, because you can't make money with a single product for $29.95. Your cost of obtaining that sale is too high.

Now, if you have a product that's designed to attract the best type of customer so you can ultimately sell them many more expensive things, then your idea for a $29.95 product is fine. It all comes back to measuring risk. You must set things up so that if you're starting a business, or if you're engaging in a particular marketing campaign, you want to ensure that you make money with bad economics – so you're not saying something like, "Gee, in order for me to at least break even on this, I have to get a 2% response." **The correct way of thinking is, "If I get an eighth of a percent response or even less, how do I still make money with this?"** Don't base your success on the best possible outcome; prepare for the worst possible outcome, and design your marketing campaign so that you still make money based on bad economics. The worst thing you can do is set your business up so that everything has to go exactly right for you to make money. Because nothing ever goes right! **Once again, you want to set it up so that if everything goes wrong, you can still make money.**

One thing that can keep you out of the red ink, so to speak, is something called "self-liquidating lead generation." You can use something like a small $5, $10, or even $50 hand-raiser that lets you attract a qualified lead. However your process is set up, they're actually paying you to mail that nice big package to them, and you're covering your costs. **Another excellent way to protect yourself against the worst case scenarios is to up-sell high-priced products every time you send out an offer** – any offer. In fact, one of the most effective ways to increase the transaction value for a product is by putting your up-sells right on the Order Form. You can offer, for example, a $297 product, an additional option for another $200, and another option for another $300. John Alanis was recently telling me about one of his products where the base price was $797, but with up-sells he got the average transaction price up to $1,200. In some campaigns, if you just offer the initial product, you might lose money.

We've all had that happen before. But if you consider the worst that can happen, you can add up-sells to the offer, and make it into a winning campaign because you increased the average transaction value.

So the mindset you should maintain when going into any marketing campaign is, "How do I set this up so that even if everything goes wrong – even if the Post Office throws half the mail away – I still make excellent profits?" **You need to consider the worst case scenarios and create plans protecting yourself against them, so if everything does happen to go right, you make a lot of money and you're happy**. But if everything goes wrong (and something almost always is going to go wrong), you're still going to make money and you're going to do okay.

Certainly, you should always be thinking positively about your business, <u>but you need to be realistic too</u>. **No sitting around the office, affirming away, while ignoring the reality of hard work and preparation**; that's just stupid, because eventually that kind of behavior will come back and bite you. Most of us realize that, on a conscious level, but it's easy to fall into the optimism trap.

Even if you're still working away on marketing formulas, or working hard on the numbers and trying to figure out what you need to do to make a profit, or just thinking through marketing scenarios, it's human nature to want to make things a little rosier than they really are. So we have a tendency to skew the numbers high, and so we think, "Yeah, I might get a 5% response," and we look at all those numbers and say, "Wow, that'd be great!"

But that's not necessarily reality. Like this principle says, we need to be thinking the other way – **we need to be thinking worst-case scenario**. What happens if the offer absolutely does horribly? What if only one out of a thousand people you mail this offer to responds? That's a tenth of a percent. Can you make a profit there? Better yet, how can you make a profit there? How can you make that scenario work? Anything that does better than you expect is always great. But plan for the worst-case scenarios, and then, when you do better than the worst case, you're still okay. **You don't want to plan for the best case scenarios, and expect to have all those numbers be exactly what you need, and then have the worst case hit**.

Going into something like this with high expectations and then falling absolutely flat can be devastating. I see this happen a lot, with marketers who fall in love with their product – something I've already cautioned you against. **They make an optimistic offer, and don't even consider that the offer might not be that well received.** The next thing they know it tanks, and they've not only lost a lot of money, they're an emotional basket case because they've been so disappointed.

It's so easy to avoid this problem by offering your customers as many up-sells as possible. We've all encountered the principle before in our own lives: it's like when you buy a burger at a fast food joint and they ask you, "Hey, do you want fries with that?" Up-selling your own products follows the same principle.

You can start by up-selling on your Order Form. List your up-sell offer right there on the Order Form as an option. Let's say your initial package is $149; that's your product price point. Yet you know that everybody who buys that is going to receive the offer for your $1,500 package. Well, go ahead and put the $1,500 package as an option right on the initial Order Form. Maybe spend a paragraph or two – but not a whole lot of space – in your sales letter talking about the bigger package you have. **It usually works out that a small percentage of prospects will chose that option, which helps you increase your chances of offsetting your mailing expenses in the worst case scenario.**

Once again, I'm going to use my friend Chris Hollinger as an example. When he and his wife Kim first started out, the highest-level website they were selling went for $1297. Coming from a Midwestern point of view, he said to himself, "Twelve hundred and ninety-seven dollars…I'd never pay that!" Well, guess what? About 99% of the people who purchased from Chris did pay for that top-of-the-line website! **You need to list your different pricing levels – because despite what you think people are going to buy, you'll invariably have some people who will want the highest level product you're offering.** You must make it available for them, or you'll lose a lot of the money you should have made.

I call this type of high-dollar product a "slack adjuster." **Properly defined, a slack adjuster is a product or service that's sufficiently high in price so all you need to do is make one sale to tighten up all your sales' slack and cover all your expenses.** Because, everything always costs more than you think it will. Remember how that theme park entrepreneur I talked about in Chapter 5 was blindsided by expenses that were double what he expected? It should have cost him $15 million; instead, it cost $30 million. You probably won't have that kind of cost overrun, but remember that everything's more expensive than expected. **A high-ticket item in your product mix, one that you regularly offer as an option to your customers, will more than make up for any losses that are incurred along the way, or any extra expenses you didn't factor in.**

Here's another point you should keep in mind. **As long as you're selling these items first and foremost to the customers that you have the best relationships with, you'll never lose money!**

You must segment your list and work with your best customers first. That list segment becomes your testing ground. Every time you come up with some new product, service, or promotion, you go to that smaller group of best people with it first. They know you, they trust you, and there's a relationship built with you. Even if they don't go crazy over what you're offering, at least you know they're going to buy in sufficient numbers that you never have to worry about losing money.

Be Cautious, But Optimistic

One last thing before we move on to the next chapter. In Chapter 4, when I discussed *The Secret*, I told you that affirmation is useless without hard work. I really mean that, but I don't want to imply for one second that attitude doesn't matter. Of course it does. **Part of what being a ruthless marketer is all about is attitude!** Even as you're preparing for the absolute worst that can happen, you don't want to be pessimistic. **Being ruthless is all about envisioning the good things that can happen while planning logically to stave off the bad things.**

My favorite Robert J. Ringer book is called *Million-Dollar Habits*. Ringer talks about developing a positive attitude based on factoring in a negative outcome, and he offers a four-step process for doing so. **The first step is to expect problems.** You're not looking for some false world where everything always works out the way you want it to, where everything always comes together smoothly. You need to know in advance that things are going to go wrong, and have contingencies in place just in case they do. If you have a solid plan drawn up in advance, you're better organized. Then, if things do go wrong, you're in a much more powerful position.

The second step is to find something good within those problems you encounter. Call this the black cloud's silver lining. We can all look back in our past and see terrible things; usually we can see some good that came out of them, even though back when we were going through them, we couldn't see anything good. Ringer suggests that if something unexpected goes wrong with your life or business, you try to find those good outcomes more quickly, right now, instead of waiting for five or ten years down the road.

The third step is simply taking action. Often, people become immobilized by their problems; they get what our friend Ken Pedersen calls "vapor locked:" so caught up in their problems, that all of a sudden they lose their edge. Instead of letting that happen to you, keep moving forward. Even if it's in the wrong direction, at least you're not stuck in the same hole.

The fourth thing is a little bit hard to describe, because it's slightly metaphysical, somewhat in the realm of *The Secret*. **You need to realize that as long as you do those first three things, good things will happen.** Fortune favors the prepared person who continues to take positive action in spite of all the setbacks. Don't expect the world to be perfect; find ways to take advantage of unexpected occurrences that you might normally term failures; take action – and you'll eventually get where you're going.

Good things do happen to people who keep getting back up every time they get their butts kicked. They refuse to give up. They refuse to quit. We all know people like that. I have a friend I call "the young King Midas." Well, all successful entrepreneurs have a little bit of that King Midas in them. They get lucky because they keep moving forward and make their own luck.

CHAPTER TEN

"But Be Willing to Take a Few Chances"

I've already devoted a whole chapter to preparing for the worst possible outcome. Now I'm going to talk about the corollary, which ties in perfectly with everything else I've been saying. And that's this: **the greatest risk in this or any business is to hold back and play it safe**. That's not to say you should put it all on the line on a sucker bet, but you shouldn't be afraid to put it all on the line for a calculated risk that can result in riches if it pays off. Remember what I talked about in Chapter 5? <u>You have to be audacious – that's what separates the sheep from the goats in business</u>. But, there's more to it than that.

I run into a lot of entrepreneurs who never reach their fullest potential because they're far too conservative. They're not risking enough. Their goals are either too small, or are more like wishes or fantasies, than anything real. Here's what I mean by that. **Lots of people want to make millions of dollars, but when you ask them about their strategies, their plans for making all that money, it turns out they don't have any**. In fact, they haven't thought through very much at all yet.

On the other hand, the people who win big on a consistent basis are those who are the most committed. They're willing to seek out the kinds of things from which other entrepreurs run. They've got more problems, pressures, obligations, commitments, deadlines, and all kinds of headaches and hassles that most sane people would ever want. But they're also doing all kinds of wild and innovative things that are consistently bringing in huge sums of money, and they eventually develop the skills necessary to deal with all the problems and challenges that are facing them.

Most people dream of making millions of dollars, but they're unwilling to face the million-dollar headaches that come with it; the successful entrepreneur faces them head on, struggles through, and learns to beat those headaches.

I've talked a lot about that, and you can bet I'll re-emphasize it again later in this book. That's because it's vitally important that you understand it properly. **You have to understand that unless you're born into money, you're going to be putting in a lot of work in order to make your first millions**. Yes, you must have a positive attitude about it, but you have to be realistic, too. Sure, there are plenty of people out there telling you that you can make millions of dollars without any headaches and hassles. I never tell people that. I won't try to convince you that you can ever make millions of dollars effortlessly. <u>The truth is that the more money you want to make, the bigger the price you're going to have to pay</u>.

I've always been impressed with the story of Steve Jobs – who, by the way, was one of Bill Gates' buddies back in the early days. There are a couple of great books about him that anyone who wants to be a serious business leader should read. One of them is called *The Journey is the Reward*, and it was written in the late 1980s. The same writer updated his Steve Job's story in early 2000, and that book is called *Icon*. **Talk about adversity!** Steve Jobs has gone through tons of adversity of every kind, and he's paid the price to get where he is. Look at where he was at the time of this writing. **In its first 10 weeks on the market, Apple Computer sold over a million iPhones at $600 a pop**. Now do the math: that's more than $600 million in one week! The guy's sitting on top of the world, right? He was one of the founders of Apple; he started his company in a garage back in the late 1970s, and look where he's taken the company. What a great success story.

But you'll find that Steve Jobs has paid a tremendous price to get where he is. He's almost gone bankrupt many times. His own company booted him out in the mid-1980s, and the people who took over proceeded to almost run the company into the ground. One of their brightest moves was to ask him to come back, years later – and out of that decision came the iMac, the iPod, the iPhone, and a lot of other incredible technology that's still to come! **It's just an amazing story – but that's typical of the lives of all entrepreneurs.** When you study those lives, you'll see that they lived full throttle and took chances and sometimes failed; but just as often, they were wildly successful. **You can use their stories, and what they've learned, as guidelines to achieve your own success.**

I'm all for measured risk, but there's risk in measured risk. **And at the end of the day, no matter how much analysis you've done, eventually you've got to sit down, get the checkbook out, and write a big check that you know could go bye-bye.** I don't like writing or authorizing huge checks for advertising or postage any more than anyone else does. Sometimes I think, "Gee, this could pay for a nice car or a big house," or something like that. I don't like the physical act of doing it, but I do it – because I know that if I don't, I won't get new customers, and I won't continue to grow my business. I won't be able to get to where it is that I want to be. I resist the urge to play it safe, which is another key entrepreneurial trait. **There will be times when you'll need to write a check and you're scared that whatever you're paying for is going to fail, but you need to do it anyway.**

Here's an example from John Alanis. In October 2006, John spent $13,000 in magazine advertising, and the advertising man wanted the money upfront. Smart guy. Not so good for

John, but in the end he measured the risk and wrote the guy a check. The ad man placed the ad like he was supposed to, but it just wasn't much of a success. It took forever for the ads to come out, and they didn't do as well as John had hoped. He didn't lose all the money, but there he was, high and dry – and wiser for the effort. Well, it's time to do it again with better magazines, because he learned a lot from his failure – and that's an important point. **Even though things didn't turn out like he hoped, and he lost some money, he learned what not to do.** He learned not to put any more money into that category of magazine ads, and from there learned what categories did work.

Even if you get hurt, you have to resist the urge to play it safe. That's not to say that you want to play it stupid, and go off the deep end of the reckless scale; that's a surer road to bankruptcy and failure than holding back. **But if you sit back and play it safe, you might as well be working for someone else, and even then you'll only have a job until the company goes bankrupt and you get fired.** The truth of the matter is, nobody's playing it safe, whether they're trying to run their own business or not. If you're an employee and have a job, you're dependent on other people to create the conditions for your continued employment. And isn't that's a little bit scary? If you ever want to make it big in business, there will come a time when you've done all your analysis, you've done all your risk assessment, and you've just got to write the check and go and see what happens, and be prepared for the worst – and the best.

About Those Headaches and All That...

Earlier, I mentioned that risk-takers have to deal with problems, pressures, obligations, commitments, deadlines, and all kinds of headaches and hassles that no sane person would ever want. That's because they're willing to take them on in order to get to all the gold hidden underneath. In my opinion, most people want to stay as comfortable as possible. The thought that they might have to go through some adversity keeps them from even trying. It's much easier to rely on somebody else for your paycheck than it is to step out there and try to make your own paycheck – even though, as I just said, there are risks in working for somebody too. In today's economy, no job is safe. There's no such thing as going to college, getting a degree, and then working for a company until you retire. That hardly happens anymore, so your best long-term bet may be entrepreneurship.

Nothing is safe, even though there's a certain comfort in having someone else take care of you and do everything for you. Why is Welfare so attractive? Or socialism? If you have someone who's willing to do everything for you, why would you want to do it yourself? You won't have any initiative, because you don't need it. When you have that kind of a setup, then the risk of having problems and pressures and obligations and deadlines and all that lessens. But entrepreneurs deal with those kinds of problems and challenges all the time.

Every day there's something happening. We all talk about the successes and the highs and the money that can result from people working hard, but that's counter-balanced with challenges like running expensive ads that don't work. **You run the risk of losing money every day, and sometimes the risk of losing everything.** Entrepreneurs face those risks so they can live that dream they want to live. Unfortunately the closest most people ever get to taking a risk (or realizing a dream, for that matter) is buying a lottery ticket occasionally.

Sometimes the biggest risk you've got to take is to decide to do something – anything – when it's not at all clear what's going to happen. I've seen a lot of business people suffer from what I call paralysis by analysis: they get so bogged down in all these different minute details and what-ifs that they can't figure out what to do, and so they just sit there and do nothing.

There comes a time when you just have to get on the horse and ride it: you've got to run those ads or do that mailing that you've been putting serious thought into. **The flipside of that, though, is not having done enough analysis in the first place**.

Have you ever listened to a radio talk show host totally destroy a caller? It almost always happens when the caller tries to sound like they know what the heck they're talking about, and then once the host starts quizzing them on it, it becomes very apparent that that they don't – and so the host smells blood, and zooms in for the kill.

It's just like that with a lot of people who want to succeed in business. **Almost invariably, if someone starts asking them specific questions about what they've been doing, it becomes readily apparent that they haven't really thought things through**. What they really want is someone to grab them by the hand and do things for them. But you cannot make this mistake. In order to succeed in business, you've got to engage that entrepreneurial spirit and say, "Okay, this is the direction I want my business to go. This is how I'm going to get there, and I'm going to be responsible for that." **Ultimately, that means that the buck stops with you. And as an entrepreneur, the buck is always going to stop with you – or it's going to leave your wallet and be gone forever.**

I know exactly what I'm talking about here, because back in mid-1980s I just wanted to make millions of dollars. That's all I cared about. I didn't want to learn how to become a good marketer, to learn how to write copy, to learn how to develop product, to deal with any problems of business and learn how to do handle them. **But, I've since learned that all that other stuff is synonymous with making millions of dollars. Ultimately, it goes back to the game concept again.** When you study the word "game," you'll find all kinds of great synonyms. Games can be fun, and they're often challenging, but they're not always easy.

As a matter of fact, the most serious athletes are the ones who work hardest and play hurt, because they take risks. I read a great story about Tony Hawk, the professional skateboarder, recently. He's scarred all over his body. He's broken just about every bone possible so far. That's a direct analogy to business. **The seasoned entrepreneurs are the ones who are paying the highest price**. Oftentimes, that price comes with problems and headaches and frustrations and challenges.

That's not to say that you can't do things to minimize all of the challenges you'll face. When people come to us and they say, "We want to make millions and millions of dollars," we often suggest, "Well, maybe you should just go for thousands first, and then tens of thousands, hundreds of thousands, and then see if you want to just stop at that point." Because a lot of people who think they want to make millions of dollars might be completely content with just a few hundred grand a year. And if you just want to make a $100,000 a year, there's a certain set of things you have to do. Similarly, if you want to make $3 million a year, there's a certain set of things you have to do; and if you want to make $30 million a year, there's another set of things you have to do. **All those sets don't necessarily overlap, but in any case you've got to get right with what you're willing to do.** For example, John Alanis is the first to admit that he's not willing to do the things to make $30 million a year; he's happy with "just" $3 million. Sure, he could do what it takes to make $30 million a year, but he doesn't want to put up with those headaches and hassles that come with it.

Another Reason to Work Hard

Most people would like to suddenly be rich. But when you just happen to win the lottery or inherit money or something like that, that doesn't mean your troubles are over – they might simply be beginning. We've all heard stories about how sudden success can ruin people; they often end up destitute, unhappy, and alone in just a few years, and you know why? **They didn't develop any skills to get that money, and they have no idea what to do with it once they have it – and they sure don't know how to hold onto it!** Not only is there a tremendous amount of self-satisfaction that comes from overcoming adversity and dealing with all the headaches that come from hard work, it teaches you how to handle the results of your success.

So let's say it takes you 10 or 20 years to accumulate the millions you've always dreamed about. Now you've got the money, and you're on top of the world. You've worked your fingers to the bone, but look at what you've become because of it! That's what makes it all worthwhile. **That's what a lot of people don't get – that the education you acquire, and the feeling of satisfaction you feel and the skills you develop, is as much of the reward as the money is.** Now the money is great, don't get me wrong! But if you ask me if I'd rather have those skills or the money, <u>I'll take the skills, and I'll take the mindset that goes with them</u>. Because if I have those, I can go get the money. If I just have the money without those, the money goes bye-bye real fast, because I'd be like Mike Tyson and buy a bunch of Ferraris and tigers and stuff, and I can't get it back. **But if I've got the skills, the mindset, the contacts, and what I've become – the self-image, the confidence – I can go get the money again.** <u>Sure, you pay a hell of a price, but the rewards that come out of it are absolutely tremendous</u>!

A man named Paul Hawken wrote a great book called *Growing a Business*, and in that book he says that the worst thing that can happen to any entrepreneur is to achieve too much success too fast – because it'll just screw up the rest of your life. Most of us would risk sudden success, of course, but it can really throw you if you don't plan very carefully how you're going to handle all that money, and how you're going to spend it. **Most people are blinded by the dollar signs, and they forget that,**

no matter how much of it there is, the money is finite – it's not going to grow unless you figure out a way to make it do so, and keep a close eye on it.

I knew a couple of guys who had a great ad, way back when the stock market was going crazy with the dot-com bubble. It was titled "*Options Trading for the Lazy and Unlucky Investor,*" and it had some great copy. Full-page ads in *Investors Business Daily* made these guys $6 million in two years. I mean, they were just printing money! And they thought it was always going to be that easy. Well, what was fueling that success was a hot product – and fueling that was the whole dot-com silliness. **When the bubble burst, their business went down with it, because people all of a sudden didn't believe in it – and it didn't work anymore.** These guys got desperate and started throwing money at different opportunities left and right, and peeing away money. They'd spend $15,000 on a test – insane stuff like that, because they'd been successful right out of the gate, and they thought that was how it would always be. It was too easy. **They didn't learn the skills they needed to overcome the problems or get a realistic view of the marketplace that would hold them in good stead later on, and so they crashed along with their market.** <u>They couldn't adapt, because they didn't know how.</u>

When you go through years of work and build on smaller successes, you develop all the skills you need to handle a big success like that when it occurs. **You understand what's going on: that it's an anomaly, that it's a hot market, and that it probably won't last forever.** So you're able to take all the money you can out of that, and keep it because you don't do stupid and naïve things. That's another good reason it's important to face those business headaches out there, and overcome them as they occur. **In the process, you're learning how the marketplace really works.**

Here's something to keep in mind: business can be considered nothing more than a series of constant failures interrupted by the occasional big success. But the big success can more than make up for the failures. When you have the proper mindset and develop the skills to overcome those intervening failures, when you get to the big success you're able to exploit it fully, to keep all the money, and move on to the next opportunity. I'd never trade the skills for just the money; there's no way. They are that valuable.

Back when we started working with Russ von Hoelscher at the beginning of our long, hard rise to where we are today, he had over 20 years of experience. And nearly every time we'd shoot a new idea to Russ, he'd just say, "No, won't work." That used to really upset me. But now, I find myself doing the same thing with people. People come to me with all these ideas and tell them, "No, forget it. Won't work." I do it for the same reason Russ did it back then: I'm really trying to help these people! My heart is in the right place, just like his was then. We may sound abrupt or dismissive, but the fact is that years of experience have told us what works and what doesn't.

With that said, what works and what doesn't can evolve over time, for reasons that might be social, legal, or otherwise. Recently, Chris Lakey and I took two of our old promotions that we ran very successfully in the 1990s , and tried to put a new face on them and see if we could spin them around, repackage them a bit, and make some more money with them. We were both shocked to see how many specific things we had to change, because our market is so different now than it was in the '90s. As we looked things over, Chris and I kept going, "Well, we can't say that. We can't say that either! Well, holy crap, we could do that back then, and it really worked for us." We know that it worked; we've got the numbers to prove it. Only it won't work today, and this just a decade later. Things that worked phenomenally well for us in the 1990s will not work today. I didn't set it up that way. I don't like it. But it is what it is; **our market has changed and we have to change with it – or else.**

CHAPTER ELEVEN

Practice Ruthless Lead Generation

One of your biggest goals as a marketer must be lead generation – finding well-qualified people who are willing to raise their hand and say "Yes, your product sounds right for me. I'd like to know more about it." That's how you get people into your business on the front-end. How you keep them and cultivate that relationship so that you sell them more products for more and more money, is part of your back-end strategy, and it's where the real money is; I'll cover that in Chapter 12. **But the front-end is where it all starts, and that's what I'll teach you about in this chapter.**

Any lead generation is good, but if you're really ruthless, you need to make your prospective customers qualify themselves. **Basically, you're sifting the wheat from the chaff, so that you end up with a pool of prospects you're more likely to convert to customers.** The wannabes and merely interested are left by the wayside; the people you end up with are the ones who are burning to have what you've got, and are willing to spend to get it. **The best way to get these people is to spend more money on your leads. You'll reach fewer people, but they're better qualified prospects, and you'll end up making more money in the long run.**

This is something that a lot of beginning business owners really don't get. When they get into business they think, "Well, I want to sell to everybody; the world is my market." **But if you want to sell to everybody, you're going to wind up selling to**

<u>nobody,</u> **because you can't write a sales message that's going to appeal to everyone.** <u>The most effective form of selling will always be one-on-one</u>.

I can sit down with you one-on-one, have a dialogue with you, ask you questions about what's important to you, find out what your values are, and sell you a particular product based on the feedback that you've given me. I can go on to the next person and have a similar sales presentation, but ask different questions, and sell them the same product for a completely different reason than you bought it.

In Direct Response Marketing, though, we don't have the benefit of doing the one-on-one stuff. So we have to write sales letters that appeal to a broad group of people. **The more that you can "niche" your particular group of prospects – the more you can boil it down to people who have the same hopes, dreams, desires, fears, failures and frustrations – the more successful you're going to be**. It makes sense, in your business, to spend more money to reach these better-qualified prospects, because the response you're going to get is going to be much better, and you'll end up with long-term customers willing to give you a lot of money to solve their problems

Let's say you have a product to sell to realtors. That's a kind of niche market where people think and behave the same way, though it's big, broad one. For example, while both may be realtors, there's a vast difference between a realtor who's a buyer's agent or who sells to first time homebuyers, versus a realtor who sells only high-end homes. **Their day-to-day experiences are different, and to a certain extent, their way of thinking.** Think of them as sub-niches within the wider niche market of all realtors. If you take the time and effort, and spend the money, to craft a particular marketing message for each one, you'll sell much more on both the front-end and the back-end because you targeted your sales message to get fewer but better qualified prospects. When you're able to do that, you're able to spend your marketing budget on communicating with those people more often, which gets them to give you more money.

Here's a rather extreme example. I had a consultant I was working with a few years ago whose average ticket sale is fifty grand. Every time he gets a job, he knows he'll average $50,000 cash. I was trying to educate him and help him understand how useful this concept could be to him from a marketing perspective. **How much money are you willing to spend if you know you're going to make fifty grand every time you make a new sale?** How much money are you willing to spend to get the sale? I told him, "As long as you're pre-qualifying and screening and you know that you're only working with that top of the pyramid of highly-qualified prospects, then what you must do is get radical! You must go to the bank, get some fresh, crisp, brand-new one hundred dollar bills, and put one on top of every personal letter that goes out to one of those extremely highly-qualified prospects, with the offer being that you'll follow up with a personal phone call in a few days. **The idea is, since their time is valuable, you're going to reward them for listening by giving them that hundred dollar bill so they can take the wife out to dinner or whatever.** And then you send it by Federal Express or another courier service overnight." Well, I never could get him to see that that would be worthy of a test. But don't you see the logic here?

This whole concept of spending more money to get and sell to fewer, better qualified leads gets lost on a lot of people, because the inclination is to think that you need more people to sell to – that if you just had more customers, you'd be better off. And certainly more customers is a good thing, but when you're trying to sell to someone, this concept of narrowing down your market by spending more money to reach fewer people and more qualified is much better.

More Money from Fewer People

We used to joke about how if we could just have a million people give us one dollar, we'd be instant millionaires! Obviously, it's not easy to get a million people to give you a dollar, but you know what? It's comparatively easier to get smaller groups of people to give you more money. **It's actually easier to get 10,000 people to give you a hundred bucks each; in the same way, it's easier to make a few $5,000 sales than thousands and thousands of $50 sales**. So there's a lot of truth in this concept that you can make more money by selling to smaller numbers of people.

It's all about target marketing – serving niche markets, the concept I outlined in the introduction. **The smaller the niche, the more money you can make, within certain limits, of course.** Obviously, if your niche is limited to five people, there's not a lot of marketplace there! But in general, the smaller the group of people you have to work with and the more targeted they are – the more money you can make, because you've singled them out as a group with something in common. **You know what they're looking for, you know what kinds of products and services they want, and you can make a lot of money with that small group**. That means that you do everything you can to qualify your leads. When you're throwing your fishnet out there, you want to attract the right kinds of fish, the ones who are most likely to buy your product from you. <u>You don't want to cast your net too wide, because then you're wasting your money getting leads you can't convert.</u>

So it's all about qualifying: <u>you want the biggest number of the highest-qualified leads you can get</u>. The emphasis here is on the word "qualified." You may end up with smaller, absolute numbers of people in your net, but they're more likely to buy from you. Quantity does not mean quality! Oh, sure, there's no problem generating huge numbers of leads if you want them, but **if you don't make an effort to trim that number down until you're dealing only with the highest quality leads, you're shooting yourself in the foot.**

Here's an example. Early in his marketing career, my friend Chris Hollinger ran a lead-generated program that got a lot of people to raise their hands and say, "Hey, I'm interested." But, then his conversion rate to actual sales was horrible, because they were poorly qualified for what he was selling, and nothing he could do would make them buy. **That's the bottom line right there.** <u>**If you can't convert them, you're not making any money**</u>!

So I suggested to Chris that he try to generate a pool of higher-qualified leads – and after experimenting a little, he made that work. He does it by, using what's called a $5 hand-raiser. **Basically, he'll write a lead generation mailing piece, targeting a list of people he feels would be receptive to the type of product he's trying to sell.** This is a very effective way of targeting your marketing. When you do this, you qualify your lead by the list that you buy or rent, or if you're working with a joint venture partner, what you've learned of his list after studying it. **In your piece, hit them with some very bold headlines, which you back up with a very good, logical argument about why these headlines are what they are, and what the prospect can get out of your product.** You're trying to get their attention, and once you've got it, you ask them to send you five or ten dollars so that they can get your next package filled with all kinds of great information and/or a valuable free gift.

Asking for money is an excellent way to get rid of all the people who aren't serious. Now, when someone has raised their hand and said, "I want to know more and, by the way, here's five or ten dollars," is that person a qualified lead? You bet they

---

are. That's a good model that can be directly applied to about any business. **People vote with their wallets, and that's one of the ways they qualify themselves**. You can look at getting qualified leads as making your customer actually have to jump through hoops to do business with you. **If you can get them to jump through a couple of different hoops, they've raised their hand at that point and said, "Okay, I really want to know more."** From then on, whenever you call them or send them another sales piece, they're receptive to it – as opposed to the life insurance salesman who calls them out of the blue in the middle of dinner. How receptive are you to that guy? You're not. You're hungry, and you're irritated that they've bothered you during time with your family. That's how anyone feels when they're cold-called. But, if they've raised their hand already, it's clear they want to know more about what you're selling, what you have to offer. **Give it to them, make them happy, and they often end up buying.**

As I've mentioned previously, Chris Hollinger used to be a teacher, and he was recently telling me about one of his former students. He's a real go-getter entrepreneur, dominating the decorative concrete business in the Kansas City area. **There are guys out there who have been in the concrete business for years, but he quickly dominated the market because he used online lead generation and had people from all over that area answering his very specific ads**. They were raising their hands and saying, "Hey, I'm interested in decorative concrete work." He perfected his lead generation and is generating tons of really good qualified leads. Ironically, this whole year he hasn't touched a single piece of concrete. You know what he does now? He sells those qualified leads to all his former competitors, and he makes more money now than he ever did pushing mud. **He hasn't gotten his hands dirty in the practical aspects of the business for a long time, all because he understood something that his competitors didn't – and he's getting ready to launch that whole service in 37 cities across the country.** So, as you can see, qualified leads are powerful, and they can really turn your business around.

What Kind of Bait's on Your Hook?

One of my heroes is P.T. Barnum, one of history's greatest marketers. Back in the 1850s he said, "Most people are trying to catch a whale by using a minnow as bait." I love that quote, because think about it – you're out there in the deep sea, fishing for a huge whale, and you're trying to use a little minnow as bait. It isn't going to work, is it? That's even truer now than it was a century and a half ago.

But, that's the way that most people think, in a general sort of way at least, when it comes to marketing. **They're focused on the obstacles rather than the outcomes. They're looking at their costs, and trying to keep everything as inexpensive as possible. <u>That can backfire on you</u>.** Instead, you need to reverse that and spend more money to reach better qualified people. It's all about conversion. It's all about how much money you spend versus how much money you make. <u>Every sale must be bought. Most people don't realize that</u>. **There's a price that you have to pay for your sales; and paying that price includes all of your advertising and your marketing, and can cover a wide variety of other things too.** For example, as I'm this writing, my company, M.O.R.E., Inc. has a brand new promotion out there that we're testing that could be worth many tens of millions to us. It may take us a couple years of testing and re-testing and re-testing before we finally figure out how to crack the code – but there's a 30-50 million dollar business here, if we can just figure it out. Now, it may take us a while to do it, but we're going to do it! That's part of the price we'll have to pay to get the payoff down the line.

We know we're going to have to re-test and re-test over

the years. It's a huge market we're trying to reach, and figuring out the right way to do it may take us a while. So we're starting out relatively small. Notice that term "relatively." With some promotions we ask for $5 to get people to raise their hands, but in this case, we've got a $5,000 product that we're trying to sell – so in order to find qualified prospects, our first test is to try to sell them a $749 product. If that doesn't work, then we'll try to sell them a $495 package. If that doesn't work, we'll take it down to $295, then $195, or even $149 or $99. But whatever we ask for, the end goal is to sell that $5,000 package. **To take it a little bit further than that, all we're trying to do (and this is really important) is to make $1,000 off of that initial $5,000 sale.**

What does that mean? That means that we're willing to spend $4,000 to get that $5,000 sale! We can do this because there's very little hard cost involved; it's a proprietary, informational-based product where the only real cost is our time. **Plus, that $5,000 sale also has continuity revenue attached to it, and that income can be almost all profit and add up fast! We're trying to build up a nice, steady revenue stream.** There's a monthly hit to it, plus those people will be customers for life (hopefully), and we'll end up making our money that way. So we're willing to spend $4,000 to get a $5,000 sale. But we're even willing to spend a little bit more than that, because we're first making them a $749 sale. That's the first part of our strategy.

Now think about that. That's the reverse of how most people think. They're trying to make that $5,000 sale up front, and they want to keep as much of that money as possible. They're more interested in keeping $4,900 out of that $5,000 rather than figuring out how to build a long-term relationship that will flood them with money over the years. **They're shortsighted; they don't realize that every sale has to be bought, especially if you want to make more money on the back-end.** They don't realize that there's an investment that has to be made in terms of marketing dollars to make sales, and they're not thinking long-term about all of the repeat business that can come to them.

This concept with which I started this chapter, where you spend more money to reach higher qualified prospects, is crucial here. **The reason you want those higher qualified prospects is because they end up doing more business with you over a long period of time – and they end up causing you fewer customer service problems, too**. That's a little secret of our business: the better the customer, the fewer the customer service problems! The more people spend with you, the better qualified they are, because people vote with their pocketbooks. **The only way you can tell anything about a customer is through their actions, and in our business the most important action is how they spend their money**. So, you're looking for the highest qualified prospects possible, and you've got to be willing to spend more money to reach those people. You can be very aggressive with your marketing when you think like that. When you set out to do something bold like that, you end up with a kind of power that most marketers never have.

When you focus on fewer and better qualified prospects, a lot of the money you put in your pocket is going to come from saving on infrastructure. If you're trying to build a business that services 100,000 lower-end customers, you're going to be spending a tremendous amount of money on customer service and updating your database and all that type of stuff. That's why a lot of these information-marketing businesses are really what we call "power small-number businesses," where they may only have 1,000 or 2,000 customers. You can manage 2,000 customers with one employee easily, and still make them feel like they're important – which they are. But, over the lifetimes of such customers, each may be worth $3,000 or more, which brings up an important point.

The really sophisticated information marketer doesn't think in terms of present revenue – i.e., "How much can I get today?" Because when you get a customer in the door, you know that if you do this right – if you have back-end products, and coaching programs, and services and continuity to sell them – then when they come in the door, you know that over "x" number of years they're going to be worth a certain amount of money to you. When you get a customer in the door today, you've just put, say, $3,000 in your bank account in the future. And so you have future money coming in. When you start to think like that, you start making decisions to bring a maximum number of customers in because you know they'll pay off down the road, which will cause you to do vastly different things than if you're just trying to get a customer in, get the money out of them, and that's that.

So think in terms of customers. Sure, you may lose money today; you may tell yourself in the evening, "Well, that was a bad day; revenue wasn't good. But hey, I got 26 new customers! It was really a good day!" **That's because you know that over the long run with the right marketing, those customers are going to pay off**. And so it re-orients your thinking away from the average business owner who thinks in terms of dollars per second to how many new customers you acquire, how much they're worth, and what you can do to make them worth more. It's a very important way to think in this business, and it's what separates the "also rans" from the few who are really successful.

Here's a good example of the concept. My step daughter – who happens to be Chris Lakey's wife – is into scrapbooking. That's a huge niche today, by the way. There's a store in our town owned by a small entrepreneur who serves that niche, and carries other arts and crafts supplies. The lady who opened that store is having trouble competing with Wal-Mart, just as a lot of people are. Wal-Mart buys in massive quantities, so it can sell things cheaper than a regular Mom-and-Pop shop can. There's a certain kit that scrapbookers use that Wal-Mart has for about $60, while the scrapbooking store has it for $89. She just can't buy them cheaper straight from the supplier, so she ought to be buying them from Wal-Mart and selling them for the same price – or even less! She won't make any money off them, but she'll draw people into her store, where there are other items they're going to buy while they're there. Just by thinking things through a little bit, and thinking longer than the short-term, she could survive the Wal-Mart onslaught. **The key is to get customers used to buying from her and to turn them into repeat, long-term customers.** When you do that, they're going to continue buying those products from you, and they'll buy other products while they're in your store.

It's just a matter of changing your thinking a little. **Don't think about making a sale right now; think about the lifetime value of that customer.** If you've got a good business model based on the long-term value of a customer, you can lose money on an initial sale and make it up on the back-end on all the additional business with that client after they become a good customer. **That's a form of practical lead generation; you're getting people to raise their hands and buy more from you by using what we call a loss leader.** You may be losing a little bit on the front end, but you're gaining a good customer. And consider this: even if you spend $4,000 to ultimately make $5,000, that's a heck of a profit. Investment bankers would kill to make a 25 percent return! **You can make these killer profits by continuing to build your customer relationship, and continuing to offer more products and services to the highly-qualified client you spent all that money to acquire.**

Don't Be a Passive Pushover!

If you don't maintain your aggressive, ruthless marketing

stance, and go after the best possible clients using the right bait for that whale you want to land, you run the risk of becoming the exact opposite of what you need to be: a passive pushover. Let me give you an example. Twelve miles from my headquarters in Goessel, Kansas is a little town called Hillsboro. They had a little Ben Franklin store downtown on Main Street that was there forever until a company called Alco decided to move in. Alco's kind of like a mini-Wal-Mart; Hillsboro's a real small town, and Wal-Mart can't go into those small towns anymore, but Alco can. **Well, as soon as Alco made the announcement that they were coming to Hillsboro, the guy who'd owned that Ben Franklin for 30 years put a "Going Out of Business" sign on his window**. I was shocked! I said to him, "Look, they're not even going to open for ten more months. What are you doing?"

And he said, "Well, I can't compete with Alco." And that was it. He just gave up, because he was a passive pushover. **Most business owners are exactly like that.** As soon as their equivalent of Wal-Mart comes to town, they cry and whine like little babies, and put up their "Going Out Of Business" signs. Sorry if that sounds harsh, but it's true. **If you look at the Wal-Mart (or whoever your big competitor is) and let it shake you, you're going to fail.**

Frankly, Sam Walton was a man after my own heart – a true entrepreneur, if ever there was one. He started from nothing, and built the greatest retail empire on Earth. And he knew, if anyone did, how to run a ruthless marketing attack. But at the same time, he was happy to tell his competitors how they could co-exist with him. In fact, he had a whole chapter in his book, *Made in America*, that was devoted to how you could compete against Wal-Mart. Why did he have that chapter in there? Because the way other business owners reacted to Wal-Mart's expansion upset him greatly; not the resentment or even the lawsuits – he could handle that. **What bothered him were the passive pushovers, the business owners who just gave up**

whenever Wal-Mart came to town, rather than trying to compete.

You see, Sam was a warrior – a competitor! He was an aggressive marketer. In that chapter, he said basically, **"What do you mean, you can't compete with Wal-Mart? There are only two real things Wal-Mart can beat you on: we offer great selection and great prices. But that's it!"** He went on to point out that there are all kinds of other things that people want, like customer service, and the best that Wal-Mart can do there are those greeters who meet you when you come in, and check your purchases on the way out.

That's as good as it gets at Wal-Mart. Try finding somebody to help you – it's not an easy task. And even then, a lot of them don't know what's in their own store. **There's no personal service. There's none of those things that people really want.** So if you really want to compete with a Wal-Mart, you should do what we recommended earlier for the scrapbook store – if you have to, go and get your initial widget (whatever it is) from Wal-Mart, sell it for less money than Wal-Mart is selling it for, and bring in a whole bunch of customers and then treat them like Kings and Queens. **That's ruthless lead generation: being willing to lose money at first to bring in quality customers. Once those customers are in the store, you can up-sell them on specialized niche items that Wal-Mart doesn't carry, and you can wow them with the personalized service they'll never get from Wal-Mart.** There are a million things you can do with your business that Wal-Mart could never do, because they don't specialize in the niche that you do.

I've got proof that this approach works. There was a recent article in the Wichita Eagle on just this subject – about how Wal-Mart is losing market share these days. **Slowly, people are realizing that they can get some really good deals from niche marketers for stuff that's just not available at**

Wal-Mart. Once upon a time, everybody shopped at Wal-Mart, because that's where the lowest price was, and for a while that was most important to a lot of people. It's starting to shift now, as people are starting to remember what good service is and how much they miss it. Now, they're starting to go back and do more and more business with these smaller shops and the independent retailers. That doesn't mean Wal-Mart is going to go out of business; they're probably still going to be one of the world's largest retailers. **What it means is that small businesses and local entrepreneurs are starting to realize that they can compete, <u>if they do things ruthlessly enough</u>.**

If I ran that local store with the scrapbooking supplies, I'd run ads telling people that if you're a scrapbooker, we've got this widget you need for less than Wal-Mart, and show both Wal-Mart's price and our price. If you lose a few dollars on that, so what? **The chances are that when they come into the store they're going to spend enough to make up that couple of bucks on other things while they're there.** If not the first time they visit, then maybe next week, or over the next six months. You've got to look to the future! I can't stress that enough. **Too many entrepreneurs are just lazy. They're not real marketers, they're just business owners; they don't think about strategies that can help them gain long-time, lifetime customers.** They think that you just show up, and business just happens – like the printer I talked about in the introduction. Do you think he's still in business? Heck no. You can't just sit there and wait for the world to come to you. You have to be proactive, to go out and get the customer to come to you. **Just because you're in love with your business doesn't mean anyone else is. That's actually a pretty arrogant mindset. Don't think that arrogant is the same as aggressive and ruthless; in this case, it's synonymous with "stupid."**

There's a great barbeque joint in Wichita that's been there for 10 or 15 years – but the owners recently announced that they're going out of business. Their reason? Too much competition! Too many other barbeque joints have popped up since they went into business. In other words, when they were the only gig, they felt okay. But now that they have to compete with other barbeque joints, they've decided it's not worth the effort. How sad is that? Obviously, where there's one barbeque joint is, there should be more! People want a range of choices in restaurants.

The fact that there are a lot of barbecue joints in Wichita proves that it's a good barbeque town, and that there's plenty of business to go around. **If the barbecue joint that's closing had been performing their marketing right, they would have had no problem filling their restaurant with barbeque-lovers.** And yet, here they are, going out of business, just because there are too many other barbeque places in town now – which is basically the easy thing to say. **They don't want to admit, maybe even to themselves, that they're just passive pushovers who were too lazy to rigorously and ruthlessly market their business.** What they should have done was asked questions like, "What makes our barbeque place unique? What can we do to make ourselves look different or unique, or seem different from all the other barbeque joints? What advantages can we put into the minds of the marketplace that separates us from the herd?"

What you need is a good way to bring those new customers in and absolutely embrace them with the fact that this is the kind of service, these are the kinds of ideas, these are the kinds of things you're getting from our store. **And what you're actually saying to them is, "You're not going to get this at our competition. You're not going to get this at Wal-Mart. You're only going to get it here."** You have to have the forethought to have already said to yourself, "Okay, if I'm going to sell this as a loss leader to bring people in the door, then I'm going to have a system in place that's going to embrace these new customers and make them mine." **Whatever you decide to do, you need to get** really creative when it comes to getting customers. That's what ruthless lead generation – ruthless marketing in general – is all about.

You see, from a marketing standpoint, being ruthless is the opposite of being a victim – in this case, a victim of your own unwillingness to do what needs to be done. This type of victim is somebody who is just making excuses; they've got all kinds of reasons for their failures. **More aggressive marketers don't make excuses. They're out there to make it happen.**

I read in *Forbes* about a company that does nothing but buy bankrupt businesses, and then turns them around and resells them. They've got a whole process that they use to turn them around within 18 months, and they sell them for a lot more money than they bought them for – because when they turn a business around, they really turn it around. **They're looking for a certain size of business, and the first thing they do after buying those companies for pennies on the dollar is to go in and meet with the management staff – and then fire every last one of them.** Their thinking goes like this: "Those are the guys who led the company into bankruptcy! We need a whole new style of thinking, so we need to get rid of them all." And they do, and then they bring in their managers, who train new people to think differently. **And that's really what we're talking about here with the whole subject of ruthless marketing. It's about thinking differently.**

How Thinking Differently Can Make You Rich

Here's a personal example of how thinking differently about lead generation can pull in the big bucks. As I've mentioned several times already, our first lead generation was for a little book we called "Dialing For Dollars." Our mailing

---

list – a subject that we're going to get back to in detail, incidentally – was initially generated through space advertising by running a one-sixth page ad in a national business opportunity magazine. It would probably cost you $600 now. Because it went out to people interested in business opportunities, it specifically targeted the type of people we wanted to reach. People raised their hand by listening to a recorded message, and then we sent them a sales letter which tried to make a $12.95 sale. We can't do that today very well, but remember, this was back in the late 1980s. That was the little spark that started the mighty fire for us. Only later did we start using Direct Mail and more expensive marketing methods to expand on it. **But almost from the beginning, we started doing things to do more business with our customers.** Our first initial product was a distributorship, so we could get them involved with us. They became distributors, and as we helped them succeed they did more business with us, and that was the beginning of our relationship with them.

That's one way you can build your mailing list. **You can either run ads to get leads, or you can rent mailing lists that are already on the marketplace** – lists of people who've bought products and services similar to yours from other companies.

Obviously, we've been doing this for a long time, so we've got it down to a science now, and we have a huge list of our own. But we still rent new mailing lists. Every week we test new lists, depending on our offer, and we get leads from those lists. **Sometimes the leads are free – they just have to raise their hand and say they're interested. We add a free report or a free audio program, and they send away for that**. Other times we ask for $5, $10, $15, and even as much as $20, sometimes, to get a better qualified lead, the kind we prefer. We do this on a weekly basis.

We're building two lists. All the people who request the

---

information from us become a part of our lead list. Those on the lead list who make purchases become a part of our buyers list. **The buyers list is the most important to us, of course**. Occasionally we test to our lead list, but generally if they didn't buy what we were selling at that time, we don't go back to them with new offers, unless we've got a really hot offer.

This has worked very well for us. People have called our rise phenomenal; within four years of placing that first ad, we did ten million dollars worth of business. The reason is simply this: hindsight being 20/20, **we had a hot item that was very timely**. **Without going into the specific details, we found the right product at the right time.** We had a lot of help along the way, initially from Russ von Hoelscher and then Dan Kennedy – and then we started just selling more and building relationships with our customers. Believe or not, I learned this from the carpet cleaning business I first started in 1985... That business taught me how to develop relationships with customers; the whole idea was to gain their repeats business, to keep cleaning their carpets over and over, and then to tell all their friends and relatives and neighbors.

That was the only kind of marketing I knew. What we did in the Direct Response Marketing business was a natural extension of that. **I knew that even though we'd never meet most of these people, would never even talk to them, the real money was in the relationships we built with them – so I did things to get more business from the people who initially did business with us.** <u>Ultimately, it's not a numbers game; it's a relationship game</u>. Once we got into Direct Mail our income just shot straight up, because it allowed us to reach more people in a much more effective way. **It's a fact that a customer generated through Direct Mail tends to be a much more loyal and better customer than you could attract in any other way**

My colleague John Alanis took a different approach, one

that was predicated partially on the technology available to him at the time. He developed a model, and set up his business as a kind of a test of his skill. His product is a method that men can use to get attractive women to approach them, no matter their looks, income or education. He wanted to see if he really knew and understood the model he'd developed, his vision of where his business would go, and what it was going to look like. He started with a digital eBook product and bought Google Pay-Per-Click traffic, driving people to an opt-in page to build an email list. That $29.95 eBook allowed him to test his copy, and let folks respond to him in a risk-free manner. Because Google charges your credit card two weeks after you buy the Pay-Per-Clicks, John was profitable the first day! In a sense, he was playing with house money, which is good.

After John knew that the copy worked, he started to raise his prices, and add in basic and deluxe versions, along with upsells. Then he took the copy that worked and transferred it to other media. Later, a guy contacted him who had a list of people who were similar to John's buyers, so they did a Joint Venture. John created a postcard based on the copy that worked on his website and put his name on it, sent it out, and the response was phenomenal. Now he had a postcard that he knew worked, so he decided to test it on rented names. That worked too, so he took the same copy and tested it as a full-page ad in magazines like *Grappling* and *Black Belt*.

At this stage, on the front-end, it's all about lead generation. As John's example shows, once you have copy that you know works, it's just a matter of expanding it into different media that allow you to get bigger and bigger, and then re-investing those profits. **This will generate more leads and feedback into the system.**

Creative Borrowing

One last little point before we go on to the next chapter: when you're putting together lead generation copy, don't hesitate to practice "creative borrowing." There are other words for it – some people would call it swiping, or stealing, but maybe "modeling" is a better word. I'm not advocating plagiarism by any means, but you can easily and legally use other copy as a model for your own. You're stealing ideas, which is ruthless. Call it "market research," if you like. **You're doing market research and applying it to your own copy. If nothing else, you can look at each piece and try to identify what makes that a good piece, and then figure out how you can make use of those elements.** You can use the same concept, the same ideas, the same use of headlines…even to the point of copying how each page is put together. **So, if you're unsure, but you know you need a lead generation piece, borrow liberally from the sales materials others are using to generate leads for their own product, service or company.**

CHAPTER TWELVE

"Do Less Work – Make More Money"

Do you want to make more money by working less? Well, hey, who doesn't?

The most effective way to do it is no secret: <u>you have to focus on reselling to your best customers</u>. Sounds easy, doesn't it? Well, while it can be a challenge just like any other aspect of marketing, in most cases it really is that easy, as long as you already have customers with whom you've built a good relationship. (That's the hard part.) If you handle it right, it's a perfect way to generate immediate cash whenever your business needs it, and all you have to do is keep making your customers good, solid offers.

The reason I bring this up is too many businesses don't even bother with reselling. However, this practice is absolutely essential to the back-end portion of your business, which is where you'll make most of your money if you do things right. I've seen so many retailers who always focus on making that one sale, and totally discount the lifetime value of the customer. That's just dumb. **You need to go back to your customers on a regular basis and make them new offers. It's a simple concept that so many business people forget**. They're hurting themselves by not going back to their customers and making them good offers on a regular basis, and worse, they're doing their customers a disservice.

Now, think about this. Say you have a new product or service you want to launch. **Where's the best place you could possibly test a new offer? To your existing customer base, of course!** Because I'm telling you, if you put together a brand new product, service, or opportunity and you make that offer to your best customers and they don't buy it, well, you're probably not going to be able to sell it profitably to your target market. **Because of this, your existing customer base is an excellent place to test.** If you make that offer to your best customers and it flops, that'll save you a ton of money that you don't have spend trying to sell it to brand new customers in your market. <u>The bottom line: the best pre-qualified prospects you'll ever have are the people in your customer base</u>.

Smart marketers understand this, and have a system in place to take advantage of it. A perfect example of this kind of back-end marketing would be a restaurant. Chris Hollinger was telling me recently about his morning routine. He takes his daughter to school every morning, and after he drops her off, he usually goes to this restaurant, a little greasy spoon right around the corner from his neighborhood, and has some coffee. He's a regular; they know him by name, and they know his habits. When he comes in they set him up with his coffee and his water and everything else, because they know him. **The owner of this particular restaurant does a really good job of knowing his regulars' names. He takes care of them, gives them special little deals, and lets them try stuff for free.** This keeps Chris and the other customers coming back. **The owner does this because he knows he's not going to make it without his regular customers**.

So, get in the mindset, that as you build your business, you need to focus heavily on existing customers. As you launch any new offer, test it with your best customers. Always have a set strategy in mind, and plan on what you're going to do with a brand new customer, and how you'll keep them coming back again and again. It's a simple concept that gets overlooked, and not enough marketers do it. They end being up the ones with the "Going Out of Business" signs in their front windows, or going the way of pushover…which is basically the same thing.

Constant Communication is the Key!

Probably the biggest reason you should keep reselling to your best customers, especially in this business, is one that most marketers never learn. **It's simply this: that the end-game of being in this business is the acquisition of a proprietary house list of customers who like you and who give you money whenever you ask them.** But that can't happen in a vacuum. For that asset to maintain its value, you have to constantly and consistently communicate with your customers with new offers, new products, newsletters, and new services. Here's a principle that I learned from Dan Kennedy: **for each month you don't contact them, the customer list loses one-tenth of its value, until after ten months it's basically as valuable as cold leads from the White Pages.**

And so, in addition to reselling to the customers on your list in order to get the immediate cash out of them, there's a more compelling reason to continue to make offers: <u>it upholds the value of your list</u>. Even those who don't buy into a particular offer still know that you're around. You're still contacting them, and the next time you mail them the promotion they may go ahead and buy. We mail to our customer lists relentlessly, and it makes them more valuable, because the more they buy the more likely they are to buy in the future.

When you've gotten your list fine-tuned properly, and when you keep communicating on a regular basis, **the fastest way to make money when you need it is to create an offer and mail it to your house list – to your list of existing**

---

customers. It's as simple as that, and it can be insanely profitable, assuming you've kept those relationships current. **With almost no question and almost a full guarantee, I can tell you that if you have a list of customers with whom you already have a relationship, not customers that you did business with several years ago, you could mail just about any offer that fits their needs and wants and it will make you a profit.** Now I'll admit that sometimes, it doesn't happen – but that's a rare fluke. <u>If you have your own list of existing customers who like and trust you, there's almost a 100% guarantee that if you give them a good offer for a good product or service, you'll make a profit.</u>

That's the power of focusing on reselling to your existing customers. **It's much easier to make the second, third, and fourth sale to an existing customer than it is to make the first sale to a customer who doesn't know you, doesn't like you, doesn't trust you, and has no reason to choose to buy from you over somebody else.** So building that list of customers – of people who have done business with you, know you, and trust you – is the ultimate resource to long-term profitability, because you've got that established group of people who have no problem doing business with you, since they've already done business with you in the past and have had a positive experience.

By now you might be thinking, "But what if I'm new at this, and don't have a list of existing customers I can sell to?" It's true you can't start in a vacuum, but let me say that you can apply these aggressive marketing techniques to your business from the very beginning. Earlier, I mentioned how my company got started out with a little product called "Dialing for Dollars," and how we built our stake up from just $300 to more than $10,000,000 in just four years. That sounds exciting, right – to go from broke and struggling to happily profitable? Well, it's only through hindsight that I can tell you exactly how it happened, because at the time I was too inexperienced and too caught up in the whole thing.

Basically, we had something that was very timely – it was the right product at the right time, and we rolled it out and got very aggressive. Because I'm an extremely ambitious person, once we started making millions of dollars, all I wanted to do was make millions more! It was just like throwing gasoline on a fire – the money just made me want to make more money! Which got us into more media like Direct Mail and made us more aggressive. However, I do want to say this: we got lucky, but we sort of created our own luck, too. We're the ones who spent that $300, and we had to sell one of our beat-up carpet cleaning vans to get that money. We took a risk. But we got lucky; we stumbled onto the right offer at the right time. **In large part, that, and our knowledge of superior customer service, was responsible for our tremendous early growth.**

So do you need to get lucky to be successful? Not necessarily. **What I'm trying to say here is that you need to get to know your customers, and one way to do that is by communicating with them regularly**. Most business people make the mistake, again and again, of trying to sell stuff that they're crazy about, when nobody else is. How do you avoid that? **Let your customers tell you what they want.** Research your market constantly, and communicate with your customer list by testing offers with them, and going by what works. Don't guess; don't assume you know what they want. Make an offer to a test audience, and if nobody takes you up on it, abandon it like a hot potato – even if you think it's the best thing since buttered pancakes.

I've got a good friend who's wasting his time with a stupid little product that he's all crazy about. I won't name him, because he might read this someday! But the point is, he drools whenever he talks about this product. His eyes dilate and it's like he's high, like he's intoxicated, when he's talking about his stupid little product. But nobody else cares about it – he's the only one in love with it!

I say forget all that: find out what's hot. You only want to spend your time marketing things that you know are red hot – things that people really want. Well, how do you find those items? Maybe we got lucky back in 1988, but now we find them because we go to our best customers and communicate with them to see what works. **Every time we get an idea for a new product, service or promotion, if our best customers don't go crazy over it, we blow it off.** We gauge this stuff. We watch the numbers. We let the market tell us what to do. We don't fall in love with our products; we let our customers tell us what they want. And the market is constantly changing, so you have to constantly test new things.

Because we segment our list, we know who our best customers are. If our best customers go crazy about something we throw out there, we'll test below that top segment, to the customers who haven't done as much business with us as the top guys. And if they go crazy about it, if the numbers are good…well, we have still other people at the bottom of the pyramid. This is a larger group we'd love to be our best customers, but so far they're not. And if they go crazy about it, then we start testing to lists of people in our target market who have never done business with us. That's how we find our best secrets. **If nobody likes the idea, or there's limited response, then we table it**. It's as simple as that.

So, constantly communicating with your customers, testing offers and seeing how they respond, is an almost no-risk way to make money. Did I say "almost?" No, that's wrong – it's a no-risk way to make money, period, because even if our best customers don't go crazy over something we offer, they'll always buy enough that we'll never lose money. So we never ever, ever have to worry about losing money when we go to our smaller group of best customers at the top of the pyramid, and then we just filter down. Once we get to the bottom of our customer base, which is the larger group of people who've spent less money on our offers, if those numbers still look good, then we know we can go out to people in our market with whom we have no relationship and test it further.

We're fortunate to live in this day and age, the Age of the Internet, because when you're first starting out, it's very easy to find out what people want. That's why a lot of us do a great deal of online marketing, too, and build an email list from that.

Take my friend and colleague John Alanis: whenever he comes up with an idea for a new product, he'll just send an email out to his customers and say, "Okay, fellas, I'm thinking about coming up with this product here."

He just finished doing one called "Secrets of Supreme Confidence." He told his client base, "Alright, I'm thinking about putting this product together, fellas. But I'm not a guy to waste time – so if you're not going to buy, I'm not going to waste my time creating it. Here's what I want you to do: I want you to tell me, what do you want covered in this thing? What do you want to know? I'll give you a free report about something really good if you respond to me."

So basically he gave them a bribe to get their interest – and it worked remarkable well. He got 150 or 200 responses saying, "I want this in… I want this in… I want this in… I want this in…," and there he had it right there – the outline for the product, and also what went into the sales letter. **And so when he gets around to launching this thing, which he'll do via email first, there's almost zero risk involved, because he knows that people are going to buy it.** If he'd gotten little or no response to his communication, then he wouldn't have bothered doing it. That's an excellent example of how, in this day and age, you can communicate with your customers quickly and effectively via e-mail, do some market research on the fly, and come up with products that are almost guaranteed to be winners before you even start developing them. <u>Spend some time finding out what your best customers want, and you'll find that the marriage between your offer and your market is seamless, and your profits will go up because of it.</u>

Finding the Right Product from the Get-Go

John Alanis' example is a good illustration of how effective customer communication and careful marketing research go hand in hand – in fact, sometimes they're the same things, though not always.

In our case, we couldn't do any preliminary communication with our first product, so on one hand, I suppose we did get lucky. **But on the other hand, although we didn't realize it at the time, we understood our market in a very intimate way.** You see, for years, I was that person who was sending away for every single money-making plan and program I could get my hands on, joining every Multi-Level Marketing company possible, and getting crazy about all these ideas; **so when it came time for us to enter into that marketplace after we had found a moneymaking program that really worked, we were ready.**

That's what our first "Dialing For Dollars" program was all about – it was a program that we had actually tested and tried and proven. We knew the market. We knew who the competitors were. We knew the people we were selling to, because they were just like we were. Sure, you can sell to markets that you have no real affinity with, but I think you're doing yourself a disservice, especially in the beginning, if you don't choose a market that you really understand well to begin with.

Once you've got that level of understanding, you need the right kind of product to go with it. Not just a product you love, but one you think will be very profitable. Remember my friend who's in love with his stupid product? He's got a bright, shiny object he's going to try to sell, and it's not going to work. <u>Too many people end up infatuated with products they love and others don't – and the hardest thing to do is to try to sell a product that people don't want.</u> That's the value of doing your market research and finding out what people want. Even before you start out, you can start communicating with your prospective client base – even if you don't have a product to sell.

This is one of the secrets that makes information marketing such a dynamic field, and here's how it works. **These days, when a lot of us start our information marketing businesses, we don't create or find the product first.** John Alanis is a good example: he wrote a sales letter first. He created the sales letter, he tested it, and when it was a hit he quickly created the product. Then John reworked his original product into a high-income professional product – a $3,700 product for busy professionals who just didn't have the time to look for the women of their dreams.

That thing was a monster product! The sales letter alone came to 44 pages. Let me re-emphasize – John didn't create that product first. First he sat down, wrote the lead generation piece, wrote the sales letter, and then he went and tested it with a pre-publication offer, saying, "It's going to be ready in 60 days, fellas. If you put your order in now, you'll get it in 60 days and I won't charge your credit card or cash your check before then." It ended up taking more than 60 days to put together, but that's beside the point: he was able to test it without investing in the creation first. The actual creation came after he got some orders; if he hadn't gotten those orders, he wouldn't have created it. **The point is, even if you don't have a product in hand, you can still kick your business into profitability very fast.** You may find it hard to fathom, but in many ways the product is the least relevant part of your business. The market is so much more important.

      Sometimes it can actually be good not to have a product in hand – that keeps you from doing what writers call "working on spec." The word "spec" is short for speculation. That's where you write something and toss it into the marketplace, hoping someone will publish it. Well, maybe they won't, no matter how good it is – sometimes the market doesn't need want you've got. The smart writer starts out with a kind of sales letter called a query, where they approach a publisher and say, "Hey, I've got this idea for an article. Here's what it's about, and here's how long it'll be." That's not quite a sales letter like you and I would write, because it's a one-on-one thing, but it accomplishes the same purpose. If no one is interested, the topic goes back into the idea folder and the writer moves on to something else. **So the best thing to do if you want to create a product is go get some orders.** Do a pre-publication sales letter for now, and then create the product if there's enough interest in it. <u>But be aware that you actually have to deliver the product at some point. They put you in jail if you don't.</u>

      But even before you sit down to write your pre-publication sales letter, the first thing you want to do is find a marketplace. In some ways that can be simple, or it can be overwhelming. Have you ever heard the story of the donkey between the two mangers? They both looked so tasty that he couldn't choose one to eat from, and so he starved to death. Well, if you suffer from entrepreneurial disease as I do – this affliction for which there's no cure – you might have a similar problem. **I see product opportunities all over the place, everywhere I look. I read an article in the paper, and I see a product. I'm** watching TV and the news is talking about something, and I'm thinking, "Wow, there's a product opportunity!" When you're an information marketer, like most of my friends are, all you have to do is find a group of people who have a need, or who have something wrong that they need to fix, and you've got a product opportunity. The problem is focusing on just one! If you're an information marketer, you could have 30 different information products reaching 30 different niches, all bringing you revenue despite the fact that none of them are related.

The customers who buy one might not buy any of the others, but collectively, you're making good money from all those niche markets. So being an information marketer just means being in tune with certain groups of people, and then finding products and services that those people want. **So if you don't having a specific product, you could still start right now by looking for niche markets and then finding products to satisfy them.** If you find a great market and create a sales message that communicates with that market, then eventually creating a product is not a problem.

While you need to have some of your own products eventually, an easy way to get started is by affiliating yourself with someone else and selling their product. Affiliate programs are great places to cut your marketing teeth. If you know of a niche market out there, chances are somebody on the Internet has an affiliate program you can join that would allow you to sell to that marketplace without having to create a product. Here are two good options: **Commission Junction (http://www.cj.com) is a great place to start, and so is Click Bank (http://www.clickbank.com)**. Both let you sign up for one account, and then sell thousands of different products.

So find a niche and marketplace, and find an affiliate program with a good product that you feel comfortable selling – and then all you have to do is run ads, write sales

letters, and use Pay-Per-Click advertising. A lot of people have businesses on the Internet where they're making money with niche markets without ever having products that they created themselves, because all they do is become affiliates for other people. That's a great way to get your feet wet without having to create an information product yourself.

Now, if you're going to go that route, do everything with the idea that you really do want to create a customer list. **Every time someone buys something from you, capture all the customer information you can**, because, even though you're just an affiliate for another company, you fronted the money to get them a customer, which is the most expensive part of the operation. And keep in mind the one point that I've really hammered home: the lifetime value of the customer. At some point, you may be able to make them your own customer; so even if you're someone else's affiliate, strive to build a valuable relationship with that customer, so you can come back later and make them another offer that they'll like. After all, that's the basis of making more money with less work!

CHAPTER THIRTEEN

"Practice Smart Marketing"

In this chapter, I'm going to discuss a big, broad topic that I call "Smart Marketing." It consists of ten steps that you absolutely have to master if you want to make the big bucks.

I think of Smart Marketing as a blueprint for creating a successful sales organization regardless of your product, your service, or your opportunity. I've seen many, many people come in, start a business, and then flounder and say to themselves, "Well, what is it that I need to do?" They get so caught up they get vapor locked – they don't know what to do next. This framework gives you areas on which to focus in your business in order to maximize your chance of success.

I'm going to talk about each topic in detail, but here they are in an easy-to-swallow form:

1.   Give people what they want.

2.   Develop products and services that appeal to a specific market.

3.   Make sure those items have the highest profit margin possible.

4.   Develop marketing systems that identify the right prospects and communicate the right message to them.

5.   Reach and sell to those prospects fast and make

the largest profit.

6. Resell to your customers constantly.

7. Create sales messages that build strong bonds with your customers.

8. Position yourself so you seem unique.

9. Create offensive marketing strategies that let you control the selling process.

10. Make specific offers to your customers on an ongoing basis.

Number One is giving people what they want. This seems pretty straightforward, but it's not always easy. I have a friend who's in love with his product and has put hours and hours of time into it, though hasn't really done the market research that it takes to really know if his market is going to like it. But he loves this product, so he thinks everyone else should love it. It's like having a puppy that you love – but it's the ugliest puppy in the world and no one else loves that puppy but you. You can't understand how nobody else wants that puppy, and it can be crushing.

The point is, you need to give your customers what excites them, not necessarily what excites you; that may be two different things. Aside from performing in-depth marketing research, one of the easiest ways to find out exactly what your customers want is to just ask them. That's what John Alanis did. He tailor-made a product based on what his customers told him they wanted. So are they going to buy it? Sure; they already did. In doing what he did, John took a page out of the playbook of the great Ray Kroc, the man who built McDonald's into the powerhouse it is today.

Ray Kroc once said, "Selling is the gentle art of letting the customer have it your way."

I think that's brilliant, because on one hand it says to give people what they want; and on the other, it says to give it to them your way. I think that's a testament to the concept that when you have a targeted marketplace, you can let customers have it your way because you're in control of everything. You control the selling process. You give people what you want them to have, but in that process, you're giving them what they want.

Number Two on our list is developing marketing products and services that are appealing to a specific market. Again, it comes back to knowing and having an intimate understanding of your marketplace. Most companies are doing "me too" kinds of things – they're just following the follower. The more you're aware of that, the more you'll see it. **There are exceptions, but those are the exceptions that we model after; those are the guys who look beyond the "follow-the-leader" mentality to see what their clients really want.** You need to become one of them to make the biggest profits.

Number Three is making sure those items have the largest profit margin possible. Most businesses just set their prices the way everybody else does; and since they're all selling pretty much the same kinds of things and following the follower, they don't really focus enough on creating products with high profit margins. **You need to have slack adjusters in the mix, (a high-ticket, high-profit margin product or service that gives you a BIG PAYDAY!) because you have to make money to keep the doors open.** I talked about this in Chapter 9.

Number Four is to develop marketing systems that identify the right prospect and communicate the right message to them. Again, I've covered some of this. But most business people don't even know what a marketing system is! A marketing system is simply a process that automatically attracts and resells customers again and again for you. Build it right, and it can work just like a machine.

Number Five is that you've got strive to reach, and sell, to those people fast enough to make the largest profit you possibly can. Again, most businesses don't have any real strategy for that.

It is the same way with Number Six, which is reselling. **Most business owners don't have a strategy for reselling at all; they're just sitting back waiting for it all to come to them**. They're not aggressive enough. They're not going after it. They're not trying to build strong bonds with their customers. They're not trying to position themselves to be unique, and they're certainly not making their prospects special offers on a regular basis. Again, let's go back to the barbeque joint in Wichita that's going out of business because they can't compete. I'll bet you they don't even have a mailing list of their customers. I know that Chris Lakey loves going to this place, and there are probably hundreds of people in the Wichita area who feel the same. Yet, are the owners of the barbecue place doing anything to try to identify the people who come to the restaurant again and again? **Do they maintain a mailing list, or anything like that? Do they make specific offers to their customers, or work on their positioning strategy? I doubt it. And that's one of the main reasons they're going out of business**.

Number Seven involves creating sales messages that build strong bonds with your customers. One of the underlying themes of this book so far has been what we go through as marketers to develop a relationship with our customers, and the thought process that goes into developing those relationships. It's not unlike dating, in that you're building a long-term relationship. **However, as a marketer, you want to control that business relationship much more than you would**

a dating relationship. This is an important concept, because when you're writing a sales letter or making an offer to your customers, you don't just want to make the sale in the moment. You want to do things that set the customer up for the future sale. One of the questions you should ask yourself is, "What's next?" **When you write a sales piece, be sure that it's not just to sell that product. It should also be to set them up for sales of future products, and services.**

Number Eight is to position yourself so that you seem unique. When the barbecue place I spoke of earlier decided to go out of business, they said it was because there was just too much competition in their marketplace. Well, instead of bemoaning the fact that you're up against all these other recipes and all these other locations, why not take some steps to make yourself unique? **Find something that sets you apart from your competitors. What could you do to make yourself seem unique? What steps can you take to do that, and in doing so, enhance your business?**

A lot of information-marketing businesses are built on the concept of an attractive character with which people bond. People tell me mine is: I'm the face of the business. It involves being the almost-over-the-top guy that everybody can identify with, the guy who has a likeable sense of authority. Heck, I'm just being me, but people bond with a character like that and enjoy doing business with them because it transcends the sales. They're doing business with you because they like you as a character.

John Alanis is the same way. From the very beginning, he positioned himself as the king of "Let Them Come to You." His business is to teach men how to get women to hit on them, and that makes him memorable. It's an effective way to do business. If you look at the top entrepreneurs on the block, they're all larger-than-life characters. P.T. Barnum was; Bill Gates is, and to a lesser extent, so are Michael Dell and Lee Iacocca. They all have these outrageous over-the-top personality traits. **When you**

add all that into your marketing, it really increases the relationship that you have with your customers, and it positions your business so that nobody else can knock it off.

Going back to the barbeque place one of the easiest things they could do is insert an attractive character into their marketing, and make it something like "Big Bob's Barbeque." Big Bob has an interesting story, and different put on different events, and stuff like that. You may be able to knock off everything else, but you can't knock off the character. So when customers begin to bond with this character, the relationship you have with your list really increases – and so do the sales.

One of their biggest competitors does just that. They're called Famous Dave's Barbeque. In their commercials, which they run all the time, they say stuff like "Famous Dave traveled the world for 25 years looking for the best barbeque…" to build up the character and his legend. Basically, what you find in Famous Dave's is the best-of-the-best of the seasonings and sauces he found when he toured the world looking for great barbeque. **That's how you build a story behind the brand and the people in it.** It's kind of a knock-off of the late Dave Thomas, the founder of Wendy's – and the principle worked really well with him. **He hated doing those commercials when he was doing them, but they were the most effective commercials Wendy's ever did, because it put a human face on the business.** He wasn't quite the lovable public character that he appeared to be in the commercials; in fact, he was a ruthless marketer. But, part of being a ruthless marketer was making those commercials. They really made that company.

Number Nine in the Smart Marketing list is creating offensive marketing strategies that allow you to control the selling process. I'm using "offensive" in the military or sports sense, not to mean repugnant. **Taking the offensive is part of being a**

---

ruthless marketer. **You don't just sit there and take what comes; you take the fight to the competitors.** It's all part of controlling that relationship, from lead generation to customer acquisition to the initial sale to reselling to that customer again and again. It all ties back into the concept of, what have you done to develop that relationship so that your customers will be receptive to that next sale?

And finally, Number Ten is making specific offers to your customers on an ongoing basis. In other words, you have to take them by the hand and compel them to come to you instead of waiting for them to somehow gravitate to you on their own.

One of the things that I like best about the Smart Marketing concept is that it encompasses many of the points in this entire book. It includes a lot of what I've talked about so far, and what I'm going to include in later chapters. In the end, you have ten steps here that you can consistently go back to as your business grows and develops, and you can say things like, "Okay, I need to do a better job of having a slack adjustor that increases my profit margin." Then you can get to work and ask yourself, "How am I going to correct that?" Oftentimes, as I mentioned at the beginning of the chapter, marketers just look at things and say, "Well, I don't know exactly what to do," and so they do nothing. Frankly – and I know this isn't the first time I've said this, and it won't be the last – most business people are pretty stupid when it comes to marketing. I didn't say they're stupid as people, but they are stupid as marketers. **If you want to separate the behavior from the person, say their behavior is stupid, and look no further than these ten things to understand why.** You'll find there are at least a few that they're violating or doing wrong.

This Smart Marketing list is a good guidepost to sit down with and examine your business. If something isn't going right or you want to do it better, come back to the fundamentals and take a look at what you need to fix.

CHAPTER FOURTEEN

"Challenge Yourself"

One of my favorite ruthless marketing tips is: **"Strive to increase your selling skills. Look for bigger challenges. And remember, you only become stronger by continually pushing yourself beyond your current abilities."** That's one of the tips on which I often focus in my seminars.

What this tip boils down to is the fact that the concepts you'll find in this book, or in any business seminar, aren't just going to develop themselves on their own. The people trying to teach you can speak or write until they're blue in the face, and nothing's going to happen unless you do something with the concepts they're trying to impart. **You have to pick concepts from the pile you're confronted with, and adapt them and put them into your own business – or they're useless**. And even when they're in place, you're going to have to make them work better for you. The only way that happens is if you practice them.

I guarantee you, when your own money is on the line, you're going to be sharp – or else. You're going to look at this and you're going to say, "Okay, here's what I need to do if I want to make my money back and then some." **Going back to those 10 Smart Marketing steps in Chapter 13, if you want to succeed in the marketplace to which you're going to be applying those principles, and you're going to be practicing them constantly.** Do that, and pretty soon, those principles – these strategies – are going to be a part of you; they're just going to be applied routinely to everything you do. I can assure you that's the case with me and with all the marketers I interact with on a regular basis, like the three men who spoke at the seminar on which this book is based – John Alanis, Chris Lakey, and Chris Hollinger. All four of us are confident that you can squeeze us on any aspect of marketing, so to speak, and the relevant knowledge is going to ooze out of us like water from a sponge. **We're thinking about our marketing every single day. We practice what we preach; we've thought through all the contingencies, so we always have an explanation and response for whatever's thrown at us.** We've spent many years working on and in our business, and developing all of the ways to put these methods into action.

If you look at the most successful people in any business – you'll find that many of them have a direct selling background. At some point when they were going through their formal schooling (if they did), they had a summer job selling vacuum cleaners or brushes door-to-door, or tele-marketing. **They did something that involved face-to-face, nose-to-nose, toes-to-toes selling. They took that knowledge with them and translated it into their business, so that they understood how to get customers, how to sell people, how to get patients, how to get clients. <u>That's one difference between them and the people that are barely chugging along</u>.** Similarly, in Direct Response Marketing, what we're doing is taking the sales process and putting it into leveraged media. But in order to do that you have to understand the sales process. Therefore, the more you strive to increase your selling skills and work toward bigger challenges, the more successful your business is going to be. What all this means, ultimately, is you have to keep learning and practicing what you've learned.

John Alanis recently attended a huge sales seminar in Washington, D. C. hosted by Dan Kennedy and Sydney Biddle Barrows. It was about crafting powerful sales messages. Now, if you know anything at all about marketing, you'll recognize that first name as someone who's huge in the field. The second name, Sydney Biddle Barrows, is probably a little familiar, but less so than Dan's. Well, let me help you out here: she's better known as "the Mayflower Madame." She used to run a famous brothel. John went to the event because, though it was free, he knew they were going to be selling something involving Ms. Barrows. It turned out to be a 10-week tele-seminar coaching program.

What interested John most was the offer they were going to make, and the crowd's response. He took many notes. **The biggest thing he took out of that event wasn't the coaching program. It was the structure of the selling process: how they set it up, the offer they made, and all the details they used to get people to buy.** John went just to observe, so that if he's ever in a similar environment, selling something big from the front of the room, he wants to do things as much like they did as he can.

Dan Kennedy and Ms. Barrows effectively used techniques like a price drop, a bonus session the next day for everybody who signed up, a free bonus for the first 50 people who purchased – there was a lot of good salesmanship that went into that presentation, and it was very successful. Not only does it come in handy if John ever does that big presentation, but you can also take all those notes and translate them into print copy, web copy, tele-seminars, and every other sales format to make more money.

What's at the heart of this or any business is your ability to sell something to somebody else – whether face-to-face, or through leveraged media. The more you understand, the more you study and the more you put the selling process into practice, the more financially successful you're going to be. That's why John went to the big event. This particular event was free, unlike a lot of similar events, because they wanted to get everybody in the room so they had a chance to sell them the ten-week coaching program. What they sold John was their sales process that he could duplicate.

Whether it's a paid event or not, most people go to events to listen to a speaker give a presentation, to take notes on the presentation, or the content of the speech. If there's an info product being sold, they listen to the presentation, they hear the benefits about the product or service, they decide if they want to buy it or not, and then they go back home.

But John went to this event not looking for that kind of information; instead, he was studying what they were doing from the front of the room. He was studying how they performed their presentation, how they closed the sales, what their payment structure was and how they asked people to go to the back of the room and place their order. **He was breaking down what they were doing to make money selling the product, so that he could incorporate some of those ideas into his mail campaigns, his web campaigns, any platform selling, and any situation where he's going to be able to sell using some of those powerful techniques.**

At M.O.R.E., Inc., we do the same thing. We buy a lot of products from the top marketers because we sincerely want to know what they're selling. We buy a lot more stuff because we want to see what they're doing. We get on mailing lists so we can see how they follow-up, how they sell people on their product. So there's a lot of educating that takes place, outside of just buying the information and absorbing the knowledge you're being taught. You can learn a great deal just by observing the processes, seeing how other people go about selling their products and services. It's good to attend events just to see how marketers do what they do best.

Keep Pushing

In the business world, it makes good sense to continually push yourself beyond your current abilities. Things happen in the heat of the battle, when you're pushing yourself to go, go, go, and you'll end up learning something about yourself, about your market, or about the technology that you use that you didn't before – and you'll be able to apply it in different venues. For example, when Chris Hollinger first started his business, he knew hardly anything about HTML code. That is ironic, because he sells web sites, which are based on HTML – Hypertext Markup Language. He says everything he really knows he learned just from messing around with it and playing with the code and pushing it (and himself) to see what it would do to web sites. And then, boom! He had an opportunity to say, "Okay, I can manipulate code here and actually sell a product to people because I can do this now," and it became a matter of copying and pasting code – and he made money. **In the heat of pushing himself and his abilities with web sites and web design, a whole new offer popped out of that, and it still gives him a nice profit margin.**

That's a good example of the kind of thing that can pop into view when you're pushing yourself. Many times you end up with more ideas than you have time with which to work. **Even if you don't, the goal isn't all that important; what's really important is who you become in the process of achieving your goal.** Generally, what you become is a better marketer.

This goes all the way back to the Introduction and Chapter 1 of this book, when I pointed out that a lot of what we call talent is the result of constant, unrelenting practicing of skills. Selling is a skill, and a skill is something that almost anybody can learn. There's a process, a recipe, you have to go through that most people can follow. Are some people more naturally inclined toward selling? You bet. But that doesn't have to be an excuse. Now, I'm proud of being a salesperson – although a lot of salespeople aren't. Selling has a bad connotation; hardly anyone wants to admit they're a salesperson. They'd rather call themselves marketers, simply because a few bad people have given the whole industry a bad name. But you have to get past that embarrassment! **The bottom line is, at some level, we're all salespeople: we're selling our ideas to those around us, those we want to persuade and influence**. We're all salespeople. Some people will admit it, some won't. Some are better at it than others. But marketing is really selling – and that's all it is. This is especially true with Direct Response Marketing. **It's not advertising, it's not marketing, it's salesmanship that's applied through the leverage of the media you use.** It is what the late Gary Halbert used to call "salesmanship multiplied."

The point is, we're all salespeople. We're all trying to sell something, and some of us are just more proud of it than others, and some of us will admit it more than others. How much you admit it to yourself can affect how hard you're willing to push yourself – and <u>that's the way you really make money</u>.

CHAPTER FIFTEEN

"Learn to Juggle"

Two of the things you need to learn to be an effective marketer are interrelated at a very basic level, even though, on the surface, they may appear to be contradictory. Two principles I often share with would-be entrepreneurs are, first, **"It's always good to have more projects than you can comfortably handle,"** and, second, **"One of the secrets to a great promotion is to allow yourself enough time to work on it."** You must live with it for a long enough period of time to discover the best ideas. The longer you re-work it, the stronger the ideas. <u>Sometimes the best ideas come in the beginning, but most of the time they come as the deadline approaches</u>. You must set tight deadlines. But if they're set too tight, you'll never discover some of the most powerful selling ideas.

Now, you may be thinking, "If I give myself too many projects, how am I going to be able to give the quality time to the project on which I want to work?" Here's what I'm trying to say: you want to have a bunch of things going at the same time, both in terms of how you rank them and prioritize them for completion. But you also have to be on the lookout for new opportunities that can bump one of those things out of there into the forefront, because you see that the new opportunity is worth pursuing. **The key is to have a little bit more going on than you can comfortably handle. It may be stressful and take up a lot of your time, but it's the key to success in this business, because frankly, most of the things you're going to do simply aren't going to work, though some will**. So when the three or four things that you're working on go bust, but the fifth thing pays off, you're able to continue to profit.

That's why you must always have a bunch of things going on at once. At the same time, you need to prioritize the things you work on; you want to block out enough time to effectively accomplish something on each product. Let's say you choose to work on something for two hours a day, then you're done with it. Then you start the next thing, and you work on that until you're done with it. Then you come back to them the next day. **In other words, always work on multiple projects, but give each project a reasonable amount of development time within the context of your daily schedule.** The trick is to make sure you set deadlines, because otherwise you'll just juggle projects for an endless amount of time and nothing will ever get done. But if you know that by Friday of this week you need these three projects to get done, you'll focus on them, even though you may have five or six or more that are in various stages of completion.

For example, I might have a letter where really all I've written is the headline and maybe the first few paragraphs, and it sits there and I think about it for a few days, and play with it a little bit. But I've also got these other projects, so I might spend 75% of my day working on other items. I've got a certain block of time available to spend on this project, and then I've got to put my head into this other project. **Sometimes it works that way, and sometimes it doesn't.** If you get knee-deep into a project and you're in the zone, and it comes to the end of the hour or whenever you're supposed to stop…well, don't stop. **If you're in the zone, you stay in the zone and you spill over. So there are certain freedoms within those basic restrictions.**

All in all, though, I think the trick is to be working on a bunch of projects, all at the same time. Be slightly overwhelmed with the quantity of everything you're working on, but also set deadlines to make sure that you're consistently moving projects off your desk. Otherwise, you just end up sitting there working on things you never get done. It's all about putting more on your plate than you can comfortably handle. A little discomfort is good because it forces you to stay active. What you don't want to do, ever, is get too lazy. For those who point out that it's possible to have so much stuff going that nothing gets done – in computer terms, this is called "thrashing" – I would point out that you have to learn to prioritize and to be ruthless about chopping away unprofitable (or even less profitable) items and putting them aside for a while – or even getting rid of them altogether.

You have to be constantly willing to evaluate new opportunities even if you're so busy you can't think, because an opportunity may come along that's better than the one on which you're working – even if you have time invested in the existing opportunity. **You have to be careful about that, though**: I know several marketers who like to chase bright, shiny objects, and they often think that another opportunity is better than the one they're working on because they don't evaluate it correctly. **The key skill is to correctly evaluate opportunities and prioritize them based on their Return on Investment (ROI)**. Don't get married to a project, because it just may happen that another opportunity may come up that fits into the context of your business, and you'll have to chop off the original idea and put it aside for a while. Being able to identify those new opportunities, to say no or yes to them and prioritize the ones you do accept, is a key entrepreneurial skill.

One of the aspects of being an entrepreneur that's both a blessing and a curse is that you don't have a time clock. You don't have a boss telling you when you have to be somewhere, or what you have to do. It's especially difficult when you're one of those people who just operate better under that type of regimen. **If that's the case, you absolutely need to put deadlines on certain things.** If you don't say, "Okay, I want to get this all together and have it out there by this date," the damn thing may just sit there and not get done. So at the very least, arbitrarily pick a date as your drop-dead deadline. Otherwise, your existing schedule may dictate when you actually have time to do a project. **Whatever the case, you absolutely must set deadlines so you'll be sure to put yourself to work on that project regularly.** And you know what? You'll probably get it done more quickly than you expect. The simple act of being engaged – especially in something that's rewarding and exciting – makes the time really fly by. When you come up for air, look back and say, "Okay, what did I get done on my list?" Look at the checkmarks there, and decide how productive you were. <u>And be honest with yourself about the direction that you're heading and the deadlines that you're meeting, and keep yourself on task – or you can flounder</u>.

There's self-discipline, and there's self-imposed discipline. The latter is where the idea of the deadline comes in. Let's say there's a monthly meeting you're involved in where you commit to something. You don't want to look like a schmoe at the next meeting and say, "Well, um, I didn't get all this stuff done," so you work hard and get done what you've committed to. That's self-imposed discipline. You say to yourself, "Okay, I've got this deadline, and I'm going to look like a fool if I don't finish this, so I'd better get on the ball." **Instead of just setting your deadlines, which you can't enforce, you create a self-imposed, disciplined work environment that gets you to do things**. You tell yourself, "I've gotta write this number of words by this time in the morning for this person, or I'm going to get fired." **That's self-imposed discipline. If you look for ways to impose discipline on yourself, you get a heck of a lot more done.**

Here's an example from John Alanis. His business is basically run off his laptop. But during the day, when he sits down to write copy or do just about anything productive, he disconnects the damn thing from the Internet and moves it to another room where he can't access the Internet at all. This is an example of self-imposed discipline. **You often get more done**

when you create this environment of self-imposed discipline, rather than trying to force yourself through willpower and self-discipline – which are very hard concepts even for the best of the best to wrap their brains around. If you're able to create this self-imposed disciplined environment, you'll find your productivity increases dramatically.

This is very, very important, because entrepreneurs have the freedom to sluff off all day. **If you work for yourself, you can decide when you work or when you don't work.** If it occurs to you, you could decide to hang out by the beach every day and do nothing. Or you can decide that you're going to spend twelve hours a day working your business and making sure you get things done and meet your goals. With the freedom to be able to do all those things and choose how you spend your time comes the responsibility to yourself to be productive, and to do things that will further your business.

The best thing about being self-employed is the fact that you are your own boss – and the worst thing about being self-employed is the fact that you are your own boss!

It's similar to what they say about defending yourself in court – that you've got a fool for a lawyer, because you're the worst lawyer in the world for yourself. It can be the same way when it comes to working for yourself. **When it comes to human motivation, the best advice I can give you after almost 30 years of studying all this is, find a hundred ways to motivate yourself.** Try a bunch of different things, and you'll find that different things work at different times.

Getting back to the quotes with which I started this chapter, I recognize that they're slightly contradictory in a way. But only slightly. I think the synergy between them is much more important than the slight differences. **It all comes down to the fact that if you don't want to lose any money, then you**

build a customer list and always, always focus on your best customers first, so every project you're involved in follows a logical sequence of actions. I've talked about this principle repeatedly throughout this book. **As long as you're constantly developing new things for your best customers first, you never have to worry about losing money** – because they trust you, they like you, there's a relationship with you, and they will always buy. Maybe they won't go crazy over what you're offering, but they'll at least buy in sufficient numbers so that you're trading dollars for dollars. You're not losing money. And they'll be willing to see what you come up with next, which they may very well be crazy about.

The creative process is a little different for everybody, and we all have to find what works for us and what doesn't. The only way to do that is by experimenting with lots of things. One of the things I like to do is always have a variety of projects I'm juggling. Sometimes I don't want to do them; sometimes I don't like to do them. But I have to. And you know what's interesting? **Sometimes I come up with my greatest ideas when I'm in terrible pain because I've got to do something, and all of a sudden my brain starts going in 40 million other directions that turn out to be profitable**. I start a lot of new projects just because I'm going through this terrible mental pain of forcing myself to work on a project, where it's like pulling teeth to get anything done. My brain automatically gives me good ideas as a result – maybe as compensation. **That's why I like to always have a bunch of projects in my head constantly, to put that pressure on me – because that pressure can be very, very good.**

I remember when I was a member of Dan Kennedy's Platinum Group. Out of respect for all the other members in that group (there were 15 or 18 or us), you have to sit there and listen to them one at a time as they do their presentations. Well, I found some of those presentations to be tremendously boring – which some of them would no doubt say about my presentations. Now, I don't like to sit still; I can't sit still. But part of being a member of Dan Kennedy's Platinum Group was that you had to put your butt in the seat for two days. Well, that drove me crazy! So for two days I was sitting there and I was working on all kinds of creative projects, because I was going nuts. I couldn't stand just sitting there, so I would come up with some really creative, breakthrough ideas while undergoing that that terrible "pain" of having to keep my butt in that seat.

Despite what some of us might think, we're all creative; or at least, we all start out being creative as kids. Somewhere along the line, though, that creativity is stifled. We lose that edge, or maybe society beats it out of us. Part of this whole multi-project thing I'm telling you about in this chapter is supposed to be fun; it's not supposed to be a bunch of projects that are nothing but work. The idea's not to make you groan, "Oh man, I've got too much work." **You need to focus on stuff that excites you, stuff that interests you, stuff that makes you feel alive.** I think that's what happens to a lot of business owners who end up working <u>in</u> their business instead of <u>on</u> their business. They get wrapped up in so many of the details, and then it gets to a point to where they just don't like it. It's painful, they're bored, and they've lost any creative spark. **Why are they still doing it? <u>Because it pays the bills, and that's what they do</u>.**

But let that creativity flow, and it can be amazing how 12, 14, or 16 hours can just fly by some days. Chris Hollinger tells me that if he doesn't totally lay it out there 100% and go nuts every day, he won't sleep at night. It'll bug him, or he'll have too much energy to sleep well. I can understand that. It's the kind of thing where if you want to get a good night's sleep and be any good the next day, you've got to expend that energy – whether it's physical energy or mental energy. (I can assure you that mental energy will also wear you out quickly.) **It's important to realize, too, that when you're in the zone, whatever it is**

you're doing, you shouldn't leave it until it goes by on its own. Because sometimes you'll get to working and everything will just mesh and click and come together, and it will just flow right out of you. Though, of course, often you don't get in the zone right away. I walk on the treadmill a lot. Most often it's like this: the first 10 minutes I'm forcing myself to do it. But then after about 10 minutes, I start getting into it; and by the time an hour has gone by I'm way into it, and it feels totally different. But still, those first 10 minutes I have to force myself!

The same thing can happen with work. **You may find yourself facing something late in the day, and you're tired and don't want to deal with it.** But it's a project you have to do, so you force yourself to sit down and work on it – and maybe for the first ten minutes you hate every second of it. But, more often than not, you start getting into it after a while, and the rest of that block of time goes smoothly. This is especially the case when you're working on focused activities, which all of your projects should be. As I've mentioned before, **that focus comes from having a list of customers, segmenting it into your best customers and everyone else, and focusing on creating more and more products and services that are designed to give them more of what they want.**

As far as self-discipline goes, one of our greatest secrets at M.O.R.E., Incorporated is this: we create all kinds of lead generation offers where we send out the mailing pieces first. Then the leads come in. **Well, every single day you let those leads sit there, they lose value. Because when people want something, they want it now. <u>Not tomorrow, but now</u>!** There's a tremendous sense of urgency when you've got hundreds of leads piling up and you don't yet have all the lead fulfillment put together for it. Now, all of a sudden, talk about flogging yourself! You're motivated now! We play that game with ourselves constantly, where we throw out all the lead generating stuff first, then people start requesting the information. **It ain't ready yet, but it will be in a matter of a week or so, because we could never let a lead sit for more than a week – ever.**

Think of it this way: you've got to be aware of your own mental processes. If you don't understand the fact that you have to get to Minute 11 on the days you don't start off in the zone, then you never get there. John Alanis tells me that every time he sits down to write a new sales letter, he thinks, "There's no way I can write a 20-page sales letter. It's just impossible!" I know how he feels: you're thinking that, for whatever reason, you've lost it – you'll never be able to do that again. But you can write a headline and a first sentence. If you can do that, you know that it's going to start going from there. That's John's mental process. Maybe he can't sit down to write a sales letter, but he can sit down to write that. What does he do to get past that? Sometimes he has to sit down and handwrite some old sales letters. **Or he'll read through some old copy, he'll just start writing something, and then it will catch fire.**

<u>Awareness of that mental process is very important, very powerful.</u> <u>Figuring out the things that motivate you and get you to work, helps you keep going on those days when you feel less than perfect</u> – the days you're not in the zone, which, quite frankly, is more often than not – so you're still able to be productive. If you're not aware of that mental process and start something and say, "Oh, I don't feel like doing it; I'm going to quit," then you never get it done.

Many people bypass their reluctance to get started with a "To Do" list; this may work well for you. Before you leave the office Thursday night, do your list, and then when you come into the office Friday morning, you're launched. People who use "To Do" lists this way tell me that on the days they don't do that, they go into the office and bounce from one thing to another and never really get anything done. That "To

Do" list works for them, and they need to stick with it. I do something similar: I set up all my work for the morning the night before, so it's staring me right in the face when I come in. Now, I don't always feel like getting up in the morning, but I do, because I know that those first few hours are my most productive time. I have to get up at five o'clock in the morning or I lose that most creative period. So on the mornings when I'd just rather just lay there right next to my wife and not get up, I always tell myself "To thine own self be true," and that quote from Shakespeare gets me out of bed, because I know that's what it's all about. **Just because you can get away with a lot when you're your own boss doesn't mean you're not hurting yourself when you treat yourself too easily.** <u>You have to have a mechanism in place to help you hold yourself accountable.</u>

Forcing yourself to do what you need to do is what self-discipline is all about. You've got the intellectual side and the emotional side to self-discipline. Sometimes those two sides battle each other. **We all know what we should be doing intellectually, but our emotions oftentimes don't allow us to do those things – so you've got to try to mesh those two.** <u>Self-imposed discipline is what bridges the gap.</u>

Maybe you don't work best by starting out at five in the morning like I do, but whenever you work best, you've got to set up a mechanism to force that. For example, John Alanis usually sets up his "To Do" list a week in advance, because he knows he's not going to be as productive if he doesn't. Of course, now that he's no longer in the military, he's not getting up at 5:00 AM for anything! What works best for him is to get up, go to the gym to work out physically, and then move on to the work day. His work day doesn't start, sometimes, until around noon. But he's most productive after that, and he can work late into the night – maybe to 1:00 AM or 2:00 AM – and be fantastically productive. That's because he knows himself, and he knows that if he gets up at 5:00 AM, his day is worthless – especially if he doesn't go to the gym.

This may sound like a cliché, but that's only because it's so true: everybody is different. **You have to know yourself, and mesh your work environment and schedule to your personal reality. <u>And, you have to demand more from yourself</u>!**

Every time I see the Forbes 400 list or read the story of a super-successful entrepreneur, and notice how they always seem to be back on the lists year after year, I think to myself, "Man, I'd love to see their goal sheets." Because I know that somewhere, these people have what they want to accomplish written down. Oh, maybe not 100 percent of them do, but more often than not, when someone is making a ton of money, they've got goals written down somewhere. My business plan, for example, is right there in my bathroom. That may fall into the "too much information" category for you, but I think it's a good example of how you can keep your goals where you can see them.

You have to reward yourself, too, because if no one else pats you on the back, you have to pat yourself on the back. So when you accomplish a task, you have to give yourself a little reward, even if it's just to go get a cup of coffee or do something. At the very least, allow yourself that feeling of completion, that brief feeling of accomplishment.

Too much reward can be a bad thing, of course. For example, as Chris Hollinger told me once, on a beautiful fall day he might want to be out on the lake fishing, but if he were, he'd know there were a whole bunch of things that he really needed to get done at the office – and it just wouldn't feel right. He'd feel like he was cheating himself and cheating his wife and cheating their business.

The reason he knows that feeling is because he's said, "Oh, the heck with it," and loaded the boat up in the truck and gone over to the lake and put the boat in and gone fishing, and the whole time he was catching fish, something was gnawing on him. **To really enjoy something, then, you have to make sure that the "i's" are dotted and the "t's" are crossed, and that you've taken care of your business before you go and reward yourself.** If you work very, very hard and you know you've really done your best, then when you go out there to enjoy yourself, you're completely relaxed and in the moment. You work hard, you play hard, and it feels so good! But if you haven't taken care of business, then it's worthless.

CHAPTER SIXTEEN

"Take It Step By Step"

Never, never ignore the potential for multi-step marketing in your business. It's an important aspect of building long-term customer relationships and setting up additional sales on the back-end – and it's those things that guarantee long-term success. **Whenever you sell a product, whether it's to someone on your customer list or somebody else's, that prospect should immediately become a lead to buy the next product you have to offer.** So if somebody gives you $300 for something, immediately start them on a multi-step sequence to buy more – because someone who's just spent $300 is a perfect prospect for something similar. If you start them on a new marketing sequence as soon as they buy something, it can be very profitable in the end.

Now, conversion rates between the steps in your system will vary all over the place, depend on what you're selling, how well your marketing copy is working, how hot the market is, the lists you're using, where the lead was generated, the source, and so on. There are no real norms, because there are too many variables. **The only thing you should really care about is Return on Investment – ROI. How much did you spend, versus how much you made?** A corollary to this is that you don't want to get caught up too much in response rates, because those vary widely according to the media used and all the other variables I've already mentioned.

What it comes down to, once again, is how much money you can spend to get the customer. I talked about this at length in Chapter 12, but I think it's worth re-emphasizing here, because it's a significant aspect of multi-step marketing. The guy who can spend a hundred bucks to get a customer can't do as much as the guy who can spend a thousand dollars to get the customer; that's just reality. What you want to do is engineer your business so you can afford to spend more to get the customer.

So what do you do when the customer comes in? How do you increase their lifetime value? On the initial sale, what kind of up-sells can you add to get the transaction value higher? Can you put telemarketing to work? Do you have a bounce-back offer in the initial package that gets them excited? Do you have a "thank you, send more money" letter that shows up a week later to get that transaction value up? **How can you get that money out of them faster, so that you can overcome the initial cost to get the customer, so you can go out in more places and spend more money to get more customers?** The more places you can go, the more you can spend to get a customer, the faster you can grow your business. We call this "closing the gap." There's always that gap between how much money you spend and when you actually make that money back. We're always looking for ways to make money faster so that we can be more aggressive, and more ruthless in our marketing.

Even if you've got a multi-step marketing plan in place, it's well worth the effort to sit down and analyze how effectively it helps you maximize the lifetime value of each customer. Look at ways to tweak that, by category, so you can get in the position to begin to expand your business a lot faster. **The better you can position yourself so you're profitable on the front-end or can shorten the return time of the money that you spend, the faster you can ramp your business up and roll out new products and new services that appeal to your clients**. If you do that right, you get a snowball effect, because you can get that money back faster, you can get more customers in faster, you can create the customer list faster, and you have more resources and time to spend on building those relationships and developing the back-end, <u>which is where the real money is</u>. So that's the way to think about it: How do I increase the lifetime value of my customer and shorten the time it takes me to get my initial investment back?

Let's say you move out of the normal marketing channels into radio. There are a lot of places you can try on radio: FM and AM radio all over the country, XM and Sirius satellite radio, you name it. If you can figure out how to get the economics to work in this kind of marketing venture, you can build your list so fast it's not even funny. **It's a matter of testing. It's a matter of adding up-sells. It's a matter of adding in things like telemarketing, if you need to**. If you can make your marketing plan work in that medium, you can ramp your business up just as fast as you want to go.

Then there's the Internet, of course. I've been hurt by the Internet, but I've been helped, too. You just have to know how to approach it correctly. You see, the Internet doesn't care where you are; if you've got Internet access and a cabin up in Montana, you can still do business using the multi-step model. **In fact, the Internet offers several ways to have prospects raise their hands so you can build a list, which is where the gold is in any marketing system.**

Whatever opportunity you're in right now or want to get started in, the Internet is definitely one of the most cost-effective ways to proceed. You can inexpensively run banner ads or pay-per-click ads and drive your customers to an opt-in page, where you can squeeze more information out of them. In the process of doing that, they qualify themselves. They've raised their hand. **They've put down their name and their email address, so they want to hear more – and you've hooked them. Now that they're on your list, you don't run nearly as**

high a risk of them deleting your email than if you were sending your stuff out blind. These days more than ever, people don't want stuff to show up unasked-for in their inboxes. For people to actually give you their real contact information means you've got a much better chance of converting the prospect, because they're interested in what you've got. **By forcing them to go through that opt-in page, you're qualifying them.** You may not get as many leads as you might like, but they're by far more valuable than most of the worthless internet leads that many people are trying to sell to.

Now, the trick on that opt-in page is that you want to make some pretty bold promises. You want them to say to themselves, "Okay, this looks like something I have to know more about. I'll go ahead and give them my email address and move forward." By doing that, they've qualified themselves. **So learning how opt-in pages work and getting that system set up can be insanely profitable. It's not that hard, either – trust me, you can go online and find a number of systems that will allow you to build your own opt-in pages.** And Heaven knows that there are plenty of existing opt-in pages, no matter what your market, that you can use as models. They're all over the place – and if they've been up for any length of time, you know they're working, and so you come up with one like that and you test it, tweak it, and it works.

With that in mind, the Internet is the greatest way to spy on people or get ideas. Some of the software programs you can buy, for example, just let you strip all the text out of an existing page and re-write it, leaving all the background coding intact.

There's another program called Spyfu (spyfu.com) that lets you spy on your online competitors; it'll show you all their organic search terms, the keywords, the ads they're running, how much they're paying, you name it. It's a dumb name, but it's a hell of a piece of software.

The competitive intelligence stuff out there is amazing, and it can be massively useful if you chose to work the Internet. Now, I don't know how long some of these will last, so my advice is to use them while you can. Eventually there might be laws written against them , but it's more likely that Google and the other big Internet portal sites will find a way to just block them off.

That's a simple model that works great for folks like my colleagues Chris Hollinger and John Alanis, but it may not work for everyone – especially if your business is primarily offline, like mine. Our model is equally as simple: primarily we use all Direct Mail. We've used other marketing methods over the years, but these days what works the best for us is to send out a Direct Mail offer that just gets people to raise their hand. Then we send a package that offers a product in the range of $649-749. That range can change, because we're constantly testing new things, but that's our current "sweet spot," as I call it. The next step is to follow up with a monthly continuity program. That's the model that we're using right now to bring in millions of dollars.

There's nothing complicated about our model; really, it's so simple a school kid could understand it. **We mail Direct Mail offers that just ask people to raise their hand; that's it. Our initial offer doesn't ask for any money. We just want people to raise their hand**. They send for a free Report or information that we sell to them, and then we send them our big sales letter that sells them our first package for that basic price range of under a thousand dollars, plus a monthly continuity. And then we have a Direct Mail sequence that goes out to them; right now our sequence is ten steps, so they get up to ten different pieces of mail that continue to knock on their door, sort of like a salesperson. It's all very simple – there's nothing to it. That little model has worked for us for the last three or four years; before that we used other models. We've done all different kinds of things.

John Alanis uses a different model, and it's one that's used by thousands of people. It all goes back to the old Jeff Paul model that drives people to 24-hour recorded phone messages, although John gives them the option to go to a website and get on his email list. The Jeff Paul model was basically the one we started with back in the late 1980s. That was what "Dialing For Dollars" was all about, by the way – driving people to a simple recorded message, only we were using answering machines back then. Nowadays John is using voice mail, and he's getting people to go to his website, too. **However you go about it, you need a multi-step model that helps you draw in prospects and make them customers for life. Maybe it's a two-step system – maybe it's three or more**. Whatever system you set up, whatever model you choose to use, you have to <u>aggressively go after those leads and attempt to close the largest number of sales and then re-sell them the largest number of related products and services for the longest period of time</u>.

CHAPTER SEVENTEEN

Learn to Write
Long-Form Sales Letters

Long form sales letters are an important part of most Direct Mail marketing efforts, but most people do not realize that these letters are not designed to be read word-for-word, they're designed to be skimmed. **You want your reader to be able to passively skim through your sales letter and absorb enough of your message to be sold.**

Writing these letters is very formulaic: the purpose of the headline is to get them into it. The first sentence is there to get them to read the second sentence, and so on and so forth. People tend to skip around. There's a certain set of people who are going to sit down and read everything, just as there's a certain set of people who are going to read nothing. **In between, though, there's this huge crowd of people who are going to read portions of the letter here and there.** And so with your sub-heads and pictures, (particularly on the Internet) what you want to do, is have something that stops them if they're skimming through the sales letter. For example, John Alanis might have a picture of a woman with a caption under it that gets them back into the copy. **You need to sprinkle teasers throughout your sales letters that are intended to get people back into the copy they might be skimming.** <u>The more you can get them to stop and read, the more committed they are, and the more likely they are to buy.</u>

Follow the Double Readership Path

Dan Kennedy taught me that when writing marketing copy, I needed to develop what he calls a double readership path. Here's how that works. As I've mentioned already, a few of the people who get your sales letter are going to sit down and read the whole thing; that's one readership path, so the letter has to be coherent for the people who choose to do that. But you've got to assume that they're only a small portion of your audience; by far the biggest readership path is comprised of the skimmers. They're busy, they're harried, they have a lot of distractions. **You want to be able to stop them and get them back into the text on a regular basis, so they can be sold by the time they get to the Order Form.** If you're writing copy in big block with no sub-heads, it's very intimidating to read, like a textbook. They won't be sold on that, because it doesn't get them involved in the sales process. You have to assume from the beginning that they're going to get distracted by something while they're reading, so you'd better do everything you can to get them back into the copy.

What it boils down to is this: <u>you have to fight for their attention and interest</u>. You have to overcome all the everyday headaches they face, and you have to get past all your competitors. Now, I want to emphasize that having competitors is good for your business, especially if you're in a lucrative market with lots of good prospects – but you still have to be aware of your competition, and do everything you can to get people to ignore their messages in favor of yours. **The sad reality is that people have a limited amount of attention to give. They've got all kinds of other things vying for their attention constantly, and they've most likely developed some sales resistance because they're tired, overwhelmed, and apathetic.** You're competing with all that, so you must engage them emotionally. Building these psychological messages into your sales letters can be powerful; but having said that, you have to realize that it's not always easy. I've discussed the fact that certain words provoke better imagery than others, like "ruthless" as opposed to "assertive." So when you're sitting there debating on a word to use in a headline, ask yourself, "What emotion does it invoke in my reader?" Fear and love and greed are some pretty big emotions with which you can pack your sales letters that can really increase your performance and conversion.

That's one of the reasons, by the way, that big, fat sales letters can be effective. The best example is our current Platinum Membership sales letter – it's 64 pages long. Why 64 pages? One reason is that it's selling a $5,000 package. While five grand is no big deal in other markets, for our market, that's a high price. So there's a psychological, emotional thing happening: the more money you're trying to ask people to give, in return, you'd better show them some meat. People see a 64-page sales letter and emotionally they think, "Man, there must really be some substance here." In addition to just doing what we call "killing trees" by writing a lengthy sales letter, for your higher-priced items you can add colorful inserts, CDs, even DVDs – these are especially effective for people who aren't readers. **But whatever you do, it's all designed to loop them back into the copy, and lead them to the Order Form** – which ultimately is a snapshot of the sales letter all over again, although it needs to stand on its own and be a sales piece in and of itself.

Speaking of the Order Form, here's something John Alanis tried for his. During one discussion a while back, he and I talked about the importance of confidence, and that sparked an idea in him. So he sent out an email, asking all the ladies on his list to write back and say why it's important for a man to have confidence in himself. He got a lot of responses – some of them were pretty brutal – and he put some of them on the back of the Order Form along with a nice picture of a sexy woman. This is real, true stuff, and any guy who reads that is going to pay attention to it – he's going to get involved. He'll say to himself, "Oh my God, these women…what the heck is this?" **It's an involvement device to move them back into your copy, which will help sell them on what you're asking them to buy.**

Experiment with Structure

Various structural elements of the text can also make good involvement devices, and they're often amazingly easy to use: really, regaining a person's attention may be as simple as changing the color or size of the text. **Bullets are another good example of a simple structural involvement device. They often do most of the selling in long sales letters, so you should spend a lot of time writing bullets and learning how to do it well**. Because if somebody is skimming through and they see one bullet that's really interesting to them, and they say, "I really want that one thing," then that's what closes the sale.

At my company, M.O.R.E., Incorporated, we're very cognizant of the importance of text bullets, so we use them a lot, and vary their use significantly. One thing we do is make our bullets different sizes. If our sales letter is 10-point Courier, our bullets might mostly be 10-point Courier – but we increase the size of the ones we want our readers to focus on and pay attention to. Instead of them being 10-point, we might make them 16-point. Instead of Courier, they might be Tahoma, or another font that contrasts with Courier. Doing this makes those bullets really jump out on the page. **If you've got a page, a page and a half, or two pages worth of bullets, you can really emphasize the ones that you want them to pay the most attention to by changing their size or font type; you can even put a box around an important bullet point.** Doing things like this grabs the skimmer's attention and draw them back to what you want them to read. They're naturally going to be drawn to those things that look different from the rest of the sales letter.

You also need to take the general physical structure of your text into consideration. I've read sales letters that were written in a blocky form, without even spaces between paragraphs – the writers just treat it as a normal text, like this book, and simply drop down a line whenever they start a new paragraph. They don't even indent anything. **It's all blah, like they threw up on a piece of paper.** It's just there, one page after another. So maybe they end up with an eight-page sales letter of boring text that, if they're lucky, the read-it-all folks will take a look at – whereas if they'd taken the time to format it properly for the double path of readership, that eight pages of dense, boring text might have turned into 16, 20, or 24 exciting pages.

One of the things I like to do when writing copy is keep my paragraphs short. My fellow ruthless marketer Jeff Gardner is a master at doing this. Sometimes he'll reel off several paragraphs with just one sentence each. They may be short, they may not say much all at once, but they're easy to read as you're scanning the page.

This tactic makes the page look like there's less copy on it; it makes it look like it's going to take less time to read, which in fact it does, because you have fewer words on each page. Do it right, and you can string enough of these easy-to-read pages together to form long-form sales letters that people don't mind reading. **A good rule of thumb is that if you have a paragraph that's seven lines long, break it up, otherwise most people are going to get lost in it – especially if it's drab and boring, and the font is all the same, with no subheads or bullets to read.**

I'm not trying to say your readers are stupid; they're not. But they don't have the time or the attention span to read a bunch of fine print. So if you've got a big, thick paragraph, do something to break it up, because it's going to be a lot easier for those apathetic readers to grasp. Otherwise, all the information in that big paragraph is probably going to be lost.

Repeat, Repeat, Repeat Your Message

Another thing you should keep in mind while working with the long-form sales letter is this: <u>don't be afraid to repeat the main benefits and features of your product, your service, or your opportunity over and over again, because the skimmers might not see it the first time</u>. They might not hit those benefits and features until two pages later, when they get to the next easy-to-read bulleted list.

You can't just repeat it all word-for-word – the people who follow the read-it-all readership path will catch that and get bored – so you need to work at it to make the same thing sound a little different. Ultimately, your job is to convince them that the money they're going to give you for whatever it is you're offering pales in comparison to what they're going to receive.

I've been accused of beating people over the head with my message – in fact, I've told a lot of my clients that it's a good idea repeat your message least ten times in your copy, if that's possible. **I took Dan Kennedy's double readership path, and I turned the volume up on it full blast!**

Part of the reason I do it is out of laziness. **The running joke amongst my peers is that with any of my sales letters, if you really want to figure out what I'm selling, you just read the first five out of the first 36 pages and you've got it – because I spend the rest of the pages repeating what I said in the first five.** That's true to some extent, because often I just copy, paste, copy, paste, and re-write a little bit. But then, magalogs – those catalog/magazine hybrids you see sometimes – are written in a similar way.

If you take a close look at one of those you may think, "Hey, this isn't a sales letter that flows. This is a bunch of small ads that are basically repeated over and over again." **A magalog is a patchwork quilt kind of marketing copy – but they're effective, simply because most people are going to skip around rather than read the whole thing.** The reader may miss all the stuff that's repeated on the first 16 pages, but he hits page 17, something jumps out at him, and he's sold. That's the way a good magalog works, and it's how a good sales letter works, too.

It's a matter of sitting down in the beginning and trying to spell out your best benefits, and then just trying to play off that as much as you can, covering them in different ways as you go. You never know what's going to hit somebody a certain way, which is why you look for different ways to say the same things over and over. We don't just do it in marketing. Politicians do it, and religious leaders do it. Any communicators do it – they're constantly beating people over the head with the same messages over and over again, but they repeat them in different ways.

That's why I love putting stories in a good sales letter. Even if you've said something a bunch of times already, well, you can say it again in a different way with a story about somebody. **People love to read stories, so then may resonate, whereas your point might not have in previous repetitions.** Different repetitions, in fact, will resonate with different individuals, which is why we sometimes beat our customers over the head with our messages.

Of course, this method just irritates some people – especially the people who like to read every single word. Remember, though, your copy isn't just for them. While they may gripe that you repeat yourself four or five times – which irritates them because you make them read more copy than they need to – keep this important principle in mind: **It doesn't**

---

matter who you upset, it only matters who you sell. One of Russ von Hoelscher's favorite stories he likes to tell about me is along those lines. Apparently, there was a doctor who was sitting next to Russ at one of our $5,000 seminars, and he said to Russ, "You know, I've been getting T.J.'s sales letters for years, and it just drives me crazy the way he keeps repeating himself over and over and over again. Russ, you should talk to him about that." And Russ said, "Look, how much money did you pay to attend this event?" And the guys says, "Well, um, five thousand dollars." End of story. **If he was willing to spend that much money after being irritated by my repetitiveness, then my message must have been getting through!**

You're going to offend people; accept that. You have to willingly set out with the understanding that some people are going to be upset. You can't let that bother you. **You have to continue to realize that the basic selling principle is this: The more you tell, the more you sell**. As marketers, we cannot concern ourselves with the people in our market who don't like us, who don't trust us, who don't appreciate us, who aren't going to re-buy from us again and again. **We only focus on serving the people who are our best prospects**. History has shown, through repeated testing, that the way to do that is through repetitive long-form sales letters, which will always out-pull short-form sales letters. And keep in mind that in Direct Response Marketing, when you're selling by mail, you're getting a response that's a small fraction of the entire list to which you mailed. **So you might make 80% of the people mad because you wrote the way you did – and yet you got a 20% response, and <u>it was a raving success among those folks</u>.**

We've had promotions where we've done phenomenally well when only three people out of a thousand responded! That's 0.3 percent. Now, think about that. Those other 997 people could have used our sales letters as toilet paper, or burned it, or stomped on it, or cursed it, or whatever. But even if they were absolutely, positively mad as hell about the whole thing and hated our guts, we still made millions of dollars on that promotion, because we were focused on those three out of a thousand – not the other 997. Now, obviously not all those 997 out of 1,000 were mad at us. While maybe a few of them were upset and think we did something they didn't like – like repeated ourselves seven times – that's a tiny percentage of the whole. The rest didn't really care. Maybe they just ignored our offer, or it didn't hit them at the right time, or they just weren't interested, or whatever. **You're not making everybody mad who didn't buy; they had their own reasons for not responding.** You're writing to the ones that are going to respond, not writing to the ones that won't. The problem is, you don't know exactly which three among that thousand are the ones who will buy, so you have to send to everybody on your list.

That's why you've got to repeat yourself, even if some people don't like it. It's all about salesmanship. **I like to say, "I can explain the product in two pages, but I can't sell it in two pages," and that's a truism in all forms of marketing.** That's why, when I'm writing copy, I take my time and explain repeatedly what the benefits are. If you have a sales rep working for you, you don't tell them, "Only talk for five minutes and that's it, guys. And don't repeat anything." No way! You tell them, "Do whatever it takes to make the sale!"

As long as your customers know that you're not lying to them, and that they can get their money back if they're not happy, you're fine. **That's what trust is all about, and it's the absolute bedrock upon which your customer relationships – and all the money that comes with them – are built.**

Sure, if we ever find out our sales reps are misleading people or outright lying to people, they're fired. They don't get a second chance; they're out the door no matter how good they are. But, I tell them, "As long as you're not lying to the prospects, as long as you're not misleading them and making promises that aren't true, do whatever you have to do to make the sale! If you have to keep the prospect on the phone for 90 minutes, repeating everything over and over, then keep them on the phone for 90 minutes – assuming it's a big enough sale."

Subconscious Selling

One thing to keep in mind about using long-form letters is that in large part, <u>the selling takes place on a subconscious level</u>. If you ask even the most ardent of Mail Order customers, "Would you ever buy anything from a 20-page sales letter after you've read it all the way through?", they'll all tell you no. But even so, they've all got a pile of crap that they've bought because they did just that. So it's clear that a lot of this kind of selling takes place on a very subconscious level, using tested, proven strategies. **You have to focus on what actually works to get the customer to buy, not what the customer tells you will work**. If you look at what they say versus what they actually do, you'll find you're looking at totally different things.

That's why focus groups are so worthless: the participants want to please you, so at some level – and maybe it's not even conscious – they'll lie to you about what you're testing. Consciously they think one thing, but subconsciously the selling process guides them to do another thing. **You can't base your marketing and sales messages or processes on what people say**. <u>You have to look at their behavior</u>. Like the doctor who was complaining to Russ about my redundant nature, a lot of times the people who act the most offended and gripe the most also buy the most.

CHAPTER EIGHTEEN

"Make the Internet Work for You"

The Internet is an amazing tool for spying on your competitors. It's also an amazing tool for increasing your creativity, since you've got access to an unbelievable amount of raw material with which to work. In fact, in many ways it's a copywriter's dream come true.

If you're doing market research, the 'Net comes in handy in many ways. It lets you type in keywords, see what comes up in your particular market, and see if there's any evidence of people in a market space making money with bad marketing. **When you see that, you can be confident that you can get into that marketplace and that you can do well.** The other thing is, you can also see what their back-end products are, everything else they're doing, what they're entire marketing model is, and really get a good idea of what you need to do to beat them.

But be careful: as useful as the Internet is to spy on other people, you want to be careful that they can't spy on you. On the Internet, you're extremely visible – whatever you're doing is right out there in front of everybody.

In Chapter 16, I mentioned a tool called Spyfu that lets you practice legal business espionage for $30 a month. **You just type in a website address, and it gives you all the keywords that they're buying on Google, gives you all their organic search terms, shows you the ads they're running, and tells**

you how much money they're spending. So if you're starting a keyword-based business where you're using the Pay-Per-Click track on Google, it's a great tool to spend time with. **You can go find people who are engaging in bad marketing, see what they're paying to be online, see what their ads are like, and then go beat them.** There are similar sites that provide items like the top affiliates of each website. **Why is that important?** Well, if you're crafty you can get into a similar business and go approach those affiliates with a better deal.

Another good tool to use is Alexa (Alexa.com). You can put a little Alexa toolbar on your web browser that will tell you the relative strength of traffic coming through a particular website. **If somebody's trying to sell you advertising on a website, you can go look at the website and say, "Well, there's no traffic here. I'm not going to give you any money for this." Or, you can investigate previous performance.** If someone's talking about how well they did last month, you can check to see, well, maybe they just got a quick hit; maybe the traffic rank went up and it went right back down. **Sure, there's a lot of BS on the Internet, but if used correctly, Alexa is a good way to filter out the BS people are telling you – because <u>an online ad rep cannot lie to you</u>.** You can just go look at the Alexa toolbar and say, "Listen fella, you're not getting any traffic here, so why should I give you any money to be on your website?"

Before the Internet, it took a lot of work to figure out what other people were doing. You had to get on their mailing lists; you had to be intentional about it, and use code names. If you sent an order form to a competitor and they saw your name coming across their desk, they were probably going to just toss it in the trash, and not ship you their product at all – <u>because they didn't want you spying on them any more than you wanted them spying on you.</u>

But, on the Internet it's so much easier to do research, to see what's out there, to see what other people in your marketplace are selling and how they're selling it. For example, there's a trick on Internet Explorer where you can click the "Tools" button and view the source for their HTML. **A lot of times their keywords are listed right there in their meta tags**. That doesn't necessarily mean they're running Pay-Per-Click campaigns with those keywords, but it tells you what kind of terms they're using on their site to try to attract traffic on the search engines.

Here's another interesting trick that's kind of funny, because it's very simple, yet it fools people most of the time. If you have a website and you're trying to protect it from people who are spying on your HTML, you can open your code in a Notepad file, put your pointer up at the very top left of the page, then hit the "Enter" button and just scroll it all down about a hundred lines. It'll drop it low enough that when someone goes to view your source they won't see anything on the page. Technically, they could just hit the scroll down button and scroll down far enough to see it; but most people don't think that far. To them it looks like you've done something to hide your code, but you know that it's down there.

Here's another category of information-gathering that's not quite spying. **There are several really neat programs out there called "multi-variable testing" programs. This is something that you can do on the Internet that you can't duplicate in Direct Mail**. Let's say that you have a sales letter website. Using these multi-variable testing programs, you can test six different headlines; you can test different pictures; you can test different background colors. You can even test all three at the same time. There's an algorithm that evaluates all these different variables at once, if you run enough traffic through your site; then it gives you the optimal website – something that you can't do in Direct Mail.

You can use these tools to discover some really fascinating stuff. For example, John Alanis discovered that on his opt-in page, the color that dramatically enhanced the opt-in rate was a sky blue. A black background or a gray background generated half the response that a sky blue background did. John found that adding a scan of his signature also increased response, and so did adding a graphical headline instead of a text headline. You might not realize all these things unless you make use of these multi-variable testing tools.

One of them is something called Google Analytics, which is available as a Pay-Per-Click thing. Another one is called Multi-Track Generator. They're a little bit sophisticated, now: you've got to have a webmaster install them. **But if you're doing enough numbers and generating enough traffic, these multi-variable testing tools can be truly powerful, because they can give you scientific data that you can't get anywhere else**. Once you've got a control that works, and when you've gotten to the point where you're getting enough traffic, you need to start testing with these multi-variable testing tools – and you'll discover some amazing things.

My biggest point here is that whether you're trying to do research, spy on your competition, or open up new directions for your business, the technology is out there. It exists. It's up to you whether you want to use it or not; I don't do much Internet marketing, for example, but if you do, you need to make use of these tools. You'll never know how useful they can be unless you get out there and get your hands on them, use them, and determine where they can open up avenues in your business. **You don't have to keep up with all the technology out there, just those parts that can directly affect your business**. I guarantee you: once you get comfortable with those, they're going to lead you to other technologies that you can directly apply that will affect your bottom line. But, you'll never know unless you get over any fear you might have and start using them.

CHAPTER NINETEEN

"P.T. Barnumize Every Offer"

There's no doubt about it: hype sells, whether you're a heavy-metal band like KISS or you've got some pieces of miracle plastic you're convinced will change American life as we know it.

Hype makes people sit up and take notice; it's bigger than life and lots more interesting.

The consummate marketer P.T. Barnum knew it, and marketers ever since have made it a part of their repertoire. **Take a look at any of my sales letters, and you'll notice that it's big, it's bold, it's blown up, it's explosive!** Lead generation pieces must be that way, because you absolutely, positively have to wow 'em. You have to have the whiz-bang in there to get their attention. You see this every single day.

Take a lot of TV commercials: "You must act now, because if you don't, you're going to miss out on the greatest ever super-duper cooker, slicer, manipulator you've ever seen in your life!" What they're selling is not a fancy potato peeler – but the greatest revolution in kitchen technology ever!

You absolutely have to hype your products, just like my hero P. T. Barnum would. **You don't want to lie and cheat or do anything illegal, but within that framework you must hype it up!** This works like magic. That's the reason you see it used over and over again; it helps get people to raise their hands and say, "Yeah, I want to know more," and it helps to convert those leads into sales. The marketer side of me absolutely knows that this principle works, when the other side of me doesn't like to do it sometimes – even though I know I have to. A headline in 72-point type may seem to scream at people, but that's because it needs to in order to be heard over everything else. **Every little sales letter is a salesman who's going out there into the world, and it's got to be a good salesman if you want to make any money.** To do that, it needs to get, and keep, the prospect's attention; it's got to tell them a story and engage their imagination. It does that by hyping it up. And it works.

One of the sales letters that's doing really well for us right now is headlined in 100-point type, which frankly is pretty big. There's one three-letter word in that headline, and that word is "NEW." Underneath it is the sub-head, and then underneath that is another sub-head. But it all starts out with that one word in 100-point type: "NEW." Why? **Because that's what people want!** We've tested it, and it works better that anything else we've tried so far for that offer. As you may recall, giving people what they want is point number one on the ten-step Smart Marketing process I outlined in Chapter 13. **People want something new. When you haven't seen somebody for a long time, the first thing they ask you is, "What's new?"** We all want something new. The only problem is, there's nothing new under the sun. And that's a quote from an ancient philosopher from 600 B.C. So we must make it seem as if it is new.

Because we all want something new, our job as marketers – like it, hate it, accept it, don't accept it, it doesn't matter – is to offer them that next new thing. **If you want to make the most money, you've got to P. T. Barnumize things. You've got to blow them up bigger than life.** Our tests have proven that's where the money is. Oh, maybe you don't want to show it to your mother – maybe you don't want to show it to your grandmother or your friends or neighbors – but that where the money is, like it or not.

I was reading John Alanis' headline this morning: "*The Amazing Secret of a Former Loser from Texas that Can Get You All the Girls You Want, No Matter Your Looks, Age, or Income...*" **Now, that headline is a great one, and it's as full of hype as anything you can imagine (John will back me up on this). It has to be hyped, because more and more, people have short attention spans.** That's not a reflection on their intelligence or anything – it's societal. These days, especially with the Internet and cell phones, everybody's day is nothing but one big interruption. This molds their perceptions and their entire lifestyles. Let me give you an example.

I have a friend of mine who loves old movies, and he's given me a bunch of them over the years to watch. I'm amazed at how slow those movies are compared to movies today. Oftentimes, the camera stayed on one person for quite a while. Nowadays, if you turn the sound down on your TV on a popular show, you'll see that that picture is changing constantly – in most cases, you can't even count to three before the scene changes. **Modern people are bombarded with so much information overload and so many things coming at them, and they're so used to change and instant gratification, that it's like they've all got ADD.**

So to make an impression, you've got to be their biggest interruption – because the first part of the sales process is attention. If you don't get their attention, you can't create interest and the desire to take action.

You've got to capture their attention first, and then immediately hook them in. The more outrageous, the better. I like when people see a headline and say, "What the heck is that?" Because when they do, they've just got to read more. That's really your goal. The more you can put this outrageousness, this bold, explosive stuff in your copywriting, the better. You have to cut through the cloud of everything else, because if you don't get their attention, your message is going in the garbage can or the delete file – and it's gone.

Even if this kind of hype doesn't appeal to you, keep in mind that this is what has always worked, and it's what always will work. P.T. Barnum knew it 150 years ago, and it's still true. I believe it was Dan Kennedy who said, "All business is, is applied psychology and measurement." **Well, in order to succeed you've got to understand the applied psychology and the big, bold P. T. Barnum stuff that gets people's attention**. It's simply what works.

CHAPTER TWENTY

"Never Compare Apples to Apples!"

When you're in the marketing game and you're trying to sell something, always compare apples to oranges. It's a simple idea, and yet it's one of those ideas about which most people don't know. We discovered it by accident.

Back in 1994, my company made more money during a 2½ month period than we'd ever made before. That was back when we first got involved with computer bulletin boards. **We made millions of dollars, by taking the apples of the mail order world and comparing them to the oranges of the electronic marketing world**. In our marketing copy, we spent four or five pages using examples that made it very clear how a person could make money with traditional mail order; we showed people what it would cost to run an ad, and all the problems and challenges they would incur if they did it in a traditional way.

We laid the whole thing out, then showed them that with the technology of computer bulletin boards – and later with the Internet – they could basically wipe out all those hard costs if they started selling electronically. **And because people saw the difference – the contrast – between the two ways to handle their marketing, it helped them to realize, at an emotional level, just how great this new electronic marketing world really was!** Without that apples-and-oranges contrast, people wouldn't have gotten nearly as excited as they did.

With one of our current offers, we go through a long process of showing people what they'd have to go through if they did something on their own. **We make everything very, very clear, and spell it all out. Then we offer our solution, which is, "Oh, just let us take care of everything for you."** And because we spent page after page showing them what they'd have to do if they did it all themselves, when we offer our solution, they're much more excited and happy. They understand better the value we have to offer.

Therefore, whatever it is you're selling, do as much as you can to compare it to other types of things they understand. You always want to shine the light on what you're doing, so in general, you must compare it to as many other examples as you can. **You only know how good something is when you have something else with which to compare it.** That could be anything from John Alanis' world of dating, to selling information products, or new cars. Comparisons are a good way to make your products and services look better, and to rise above everybody else's.

Let's look closer at John Alanis' marketing. One place where he likes to use the apples-and-oranges comparison is in price justification. **When you have something that's somewhat unfamiliar to somebody, one way to help them decide to buy is to compare it to something in real life that's very cheap**. So John compares one of his higher-priced products to a McDonald's burger and fries, and says (and I paraphrase loosely), "If you sit down and break it out over a year's time, this product is going to cost you $2.18 cents a day – which is half what you'll pay for a Big Mac and fries, which will only make you fat anyway. So what kind of person are you? Are you the person who's going to take action and create the life you want, or are you a Big Mac-and-fries kind of guy?" **That gives the prospect a decision to make right there, and puts a definite image in his head.** Yes, it's comparing the familiar to the unfamiliar, but it's very effective in a price justification and sales-closing way.

My company's doing exactly the same thing with our Platinum Membership in our coaching program, which is designed to help business owners make more money. **Our basic USP (Unique Selling Position) is that you can attend up to 40 different marketing workshops for about the same amount of money as many marketing experts charge for one.** Then you can get our continual, ongoing help for about the same price you pay, normally, for a daily fast-food meal. It's a way to make our price seem smaller, by comparing it to other things.

You can also make them feel a little bit guilty at the same time, because they all know they're wasting money. **One thing you can say is, "Look, any man can afford this. I can look at your expenses and see you're spending money on beer, burgers, and video games, all of which are only going to make you fat, drunk, and dumb. So you can afford this. You just have to decide what you want to spend the money on."** The idea is to make them say, "Hey, I'm not one of those beer and video games guys. I want to be a guy who's going to be successful in life."

That appeal works well in nudging prospects over the line when they're uncertain about the price. Here are the apples, sure – but how about those oranges? You're doing the thinking for them, in some ways, and helping to make your case. But that's okay – you're also helping them to see things a little more clearly. Do that properly, and some will nod and say, "Hey, that's right! I am spending all my money on beer, burgers, and video games. What the heck am I thinking?"

Chris Lakey recently wrote a sales letter where he broke out the cost by the day. It's a one-year program, and the total ends up being about eight bucks a day. It's not cheap, but you can make it seem more reasonable if you use the apples-and-oranges approach, as Chris did. You can tell someone that something costs $3,000, and that sounds like a lot of money; but when you break it down and say, "Well, this is a one-year program, so this is how much it's going to cost you per day," that can be pretty effective. After all, what's eight bucks? A couple of venti lattes at Starbucks, or the price of a first-run movie.

In Chris Lakey's letter, he compares the cost of the program to hiring someone to take care of the work for you. **The wording he uses is, "A gum-chewing, text-messaging teenager would cost you six bucks an hour, minimum, to do this work for you."** Again, he's comparing apples to oranges here. Assuming that gum-chewing, text-messaging teenager worked for you full time and had insurance and other benefits, he'd cost you maybe $20,000 a year. Or, you can hire some of the most successful entrepreneurs in the business to help you with coaching and other high-end tasks, and it's only going to cost you eight bucks a day.

So what's more attractive, $6 an hour, or $8 a day? What's going to make you more money, that minimum-wage employee or what we have to offer? You could make it even more attractive by bringing it down to the hourly level: what's better, a dollar an hour, or six? **Break it down to the lowest possible number, and that number is what sticks in people's minds instead of the $3,000 price that you're really asking**. Only when they really dig in do you ever actually tell them how much to write the check. The rest of it's all about talking up that minimum price point and convincing them that they're getting tremendous value for their money.

Outwitting the Confused Mind

One of the truisms of marketing is that a confused mind will always say no. Therefore, if you have a complicated offer and you need to get your prospects from where you believe they're at to understanding the features, benefits, and concepts of your offer, you need to make some analogies. **That's what analogies are all about – bridging the gap from where they're at to where you want them to be; from confused mind to confirmed seller.**

My colleague Chris Hollinger tells me that all teachers do this in the classroom; they look at where the majority of the class is, and build on those concepts by using things to which the kids can relate. Those analogies may vary widely from inner-city schools to rural schools, just as they do from market to market in business.

The analogies you choose depend on where you want to take them. You absolutely have to fill that gap in their mind to where they can at least see themselves profiting from the product you're offering them. It's up to you to help people understand why what you have is valuable to them, and the apples-to-oranges analogy is a great way to accomplish it.

CHAPTER TWENTY-ONE

"Always, Always Follow Up!"

As I've said repeatedly in this book, effective, long-term profitability in any business boils down to developing good relationships with your customers and reselling to them repeatedly.

If you're not following up on every sale, this isn't going to happen. And once you've made a sale, you must send them additional marketing material about your next product or service.

Plain and simply, you're losing money without a strong follow-up marketing campaign. **The secret to maximizing your sales and profits is to put a ton of pressure on your prospects by raining mail, email, phone calls and faxes on their heads, because the resulting pressure stimulates sales.** Most marketers simply aren't aggressive enough on their follow-up marketing campaigns. They're giving up on their leads far too soon, and they aren't putting enough pressure on their prospective buyers. Because of this, they're losing a ton of money that should and could be theirs. **One thing that keeps marketers from applying that pressure is that they get worried about upsetting people; I've talked about that before. But you can't worry about who you're going to offend, or you're limiting your potential profits.**

A lot of marketers have the sales process down only partially. They get high-qualified leads, and then what do they do with those leads? **They send them their offer, get the response**

back, and that's it. Let's say they get a response where 5-10% of the people who requested the information from them bought, and that's it. They either decide at that point whether the campaign lost or made money, and then they move on. Some marketers, though, have it a little more correct: they have a limited follow-up campaign. Maybe they get leads, they make sales, and then they send out a follow-up letter or two to try to get more of those sales. But then that's it.

Our principle is that you should keep calling, faxing, e-mailing and mailing follow-up offers until it becomes unprofitable to do so. How long that takes is dependent upon your offer, how strong your prospects are, and how highly-qualified your leads are. About a year ago as of this writing, we were running a campaign that had over 20 follow-up sales letters that went out after the initial package.

This was a test of a sort, and we found out that it only took six or seven follow-ups before we started seeing a loss on our investment. So we stopped sending out the subsequent sales letters. Now, keep in mind that this was the number of letters that worked for this particular campaign; it may be the right number for similar campaigns that we run, but the number for other types of campaigns we run may be different, and they may have no resemblance at all to what's necessary for your campaigns.

When running your own, you definitely must test and measure to determine the point where you stop getting a return on your advertising dollars by doing more follow-up marketing. The question becomes, at what point does it cost you more money than you make from the orders you get? But most people never bother to learn that, so essentially they're leaving money on the table.

In addition to testing, determining the right amount of pressure is somewhat subjective. Here's an example of what it

---

means for us. **Let's say we have a campaign that we're mailing, where we've got leads coming in and we're responding to them.** Let's say they're requesting a free report and a CD. They had to raise their hand and request it, and maybe send five bucks to get it. So we've got thousands of leads that have come in. What we do immediately – within 24 hours if we can – is get the material out to them. **Obviously, a certain percentage are going to respond; so within a week to 10 days after we send that initial package out, we begin our follow-up marketing.** Let's say seven days after that first package goes out, we send a second mailing package out. And then we try to send something out twice a week.

It might just be a postcard, or it might be a full Direct Mail package with a long-form sales letter and Order Form; but whatever the case, <u>we try to touch base with them twice a week until they buy</u>. Again, how long you keep at it with a particular campaign has to do with how profitable it is for you to do so.

As a strategy, raining marketing messages on your prospects' heads, as we like to call it, just means continuously staying on top of them, reminding them about our offer. There are smart ways to do it, and there are dumb ways to do it. **Doing it smartly means being creative with your follow-ups; it means not doing the same thing every time.** If you've got their email address, maybe it means that every couple days, you send them an email; or even every day. But then you also drop a package in the mail to them, or maybe it's a postcard. Sometimes it's a lumpy mail offer with something in the envelope to make it stand out so they're more likely to open it. **It's all about continuously reminding them that they still haven't purchased from you, and bringing up the main reasons why they must do it now; giving them a way to contact you or multiple ways to contact you; keeping your offer on the top of their mind.** The longer you go without communicating with them in follow-ups, the less likely they are to buy.

Ideally, the pressure's coming from them, not us. If we made them an offer and they raised their hand, then they've indicated they're at least mildly interested in our product or service. It's not so much that we're putting pressure on them to buy (although we are, by mailing to them frequently), it's mostly internal pressure that they're feeling. Every time we mail to them, they know they're interested in what we have, and the pressure can be internalized with them as in, "I've got this offer; I need to act. I'm being reminded I need to act. I need to do something about this. I either need to decide I'm not going to buy, or I need to decide to buy."

Our follow-up marketing campaigns usually last about six to eight weeks, and again that's based on how profitable it is to continue. <u>The key is to keep mailing often enough that you're reminding them consistently that they still need to do business with you</u>. **Don't think, "Well, I just sent them the offer a week ago, so I'm going to wait a couple more weeks to follow-up with them."** By that time, they're on to something else. You need to hit them with a follow-up offer quickly enough that they don't lose sight of the fact that they did request this information from you, and that they still haven't made a decision to buy. **What's more likely to get acted upon: the one mailing that gets put on the bottom of the pile and forgotten, or the multiple mailings that keep hitting you?**

Sometimes it takes a handful of contacts, or more, before the average prospect buys. Some marketers get high numbers the third time they contact the prospect; for others it's the seventh contact, (especially with email), that gets the biggest response and more conversions. But it varies for each market and offer and you learn that through testing.

Here's an example. There's a guy named Dean Cipriano who does niche marketing to the insurance field. If you get on his list, you're going to get three faxes a day from Dean – he's the King of Faxing. If you get on his list and give him all your contact info, you're going to get on his Direct Mail sequence, his email sequence, his fax sequence, and he's got all kinds of stuff that he'll send you. You'll still be getting it six months later, even if you don't buy anything. The reason Dean is doing this is because it works. It's tremendously effective. This "rain" of marketing messages cuts through all the clutter and gets them to respond.

The other thing about the multi-step, multi-media stuff is the fact that, again, it's a moving parade of interest. **In other words, you never know when something is going to happen that triggers someone's interest**. There's a percentage of the people who request information because they're interested and they're ready to buy right now, but there's a bigger percentage who are just kind of curious. So, when they get your copy they take a look, then set it aside – and then something happens and they're ready to buy. **Well, if you're not in front of them when they're ready to buy, they're going to buy from somebody else.**

Then again, there's a certain percentage of people who just won't buy the first time they get something. They won't buy the second or third time, either. It might take them seven or eight times to buy, for whatever reason. **But finally they call and say, said, "Okay, you got me! I've been thinking about it, and I read it, and you got me!"** That's just their buying mechanism; different people have different buying mechanisms. There are those people who see something and buy it immediately. There are those who see something and have to study everything about it before they buy. There are people who have to be exposed to something 18 times before the light finally comes on. **That's why you've got to keep following up with these multi-step, multi-media approaches if you want to be a truly effective marketer**.

It's a good idea to re-mail to your old leads, too, because that all loops around to the concept of lifetime value. Old leads – the people you've already established contact with who didn't buy – are another whole universe to tap in order to get more customers. Maybe you couldn't interest them on that original campaign, but they might respond the next one. So don't give up on them too soon. **You may not be profitable on the first transaction, but you know that if you do things carefully, the money you spend is going to be made up on the back-end**.

Here's a case in point. When we first started working with Dan Kennedy in 1993, he produced an infomercial for us. It was a great infomercial, a lead-generation type where interested people could send in for a free video and report. At that time, we ran into a problem that we often encounter. **We rarely have any trouble generating leads; quite the opposite, in fact. We can generate all the leads in the world, but so what?** <u>The important thing is converting those leads profitably</u>. We ran this infomercial, tested it in 14 different cities, and it generated a lot of leads – as usual. I tried everything I could to convert those leads, but I was having some severe problems doing so.

One day, we met with Dan and took him out to lunch. I kept showing him all these things I was doing to try to convert the leads we'd gotten from this infomercial, and no matter what I said, Dan always said the same thing: "You're giving up on them too soon." Dan's always been blunt and straightforward that way. Well, I told him, "But Dan, I'm doing this and this and this." And he kept saying, "So? You're giving up on them too soon."

Man, was I ticked off! **I was so angry and frustrated, and I didn't want to believe what he told me.** But ultimately, the experience taught me a valuable lesson – and that's when I started becoming a firm believer in the principal of following up with prospects. I saw through that anger, and started really thinking it through – and realized he was right. I was giving up on those leads too soon. I give the same advice now to other marketers.

Patience is a Marketing Virtue

When you're working with a highly-qualified prospect who has shown an interest in what you are offering, then you're doing them a disservice if you don't do everything possible to follow up as often as possible. Obviously you're offering something that can help them and add value to their life and is real and solid, or you shouldn't be pushing it in the first place. **Now, there may be some lag time before you see results; you can't expect instant gratification, especially if you're working through print ads.**

Let me give you a perfect example of that, courtesy of my colleague John Alanis. He has a pretty good, long follow-up sequence in both Direct Mail and email. He ran an ad in Iron Man Magazine, and the cost was steep: $2,200. Well, it did okay, but just okay, so he was a little disappointed in it. **Eight months later, John went back and looked at the whole marketing campaign and realized, "This thing finally turned out to be profitable."** In fact, it turned out to be really profitable – but it took eight months of follow-up for it to get there.

Let's say you're able to run in a hundred magazines a month, and all you made on each magazine was a thousand dollars worth of lifetime customer value. Well, that's a hundred thousand dollars a month, net. With the right follow up, it may still take a long time for it to pay off, but it will eventually pay off. **And so when evaluating some of these methods, especially the offline methods, just recall that success won't happen overnight.**

Remember, it took John eight long months for that ad to become super-profitable. But those eight months are going to pass eventually. <u>So never give up on your leads too early, because they've got a lot of residual value</u>. Yes, it takes a while, and part of the game is trying to shorten so that you can manage your cash flow and expand faster. But the money is really made in the relentless way you keep trying to re-sell to your prospects and customers.

CHAPTER TWENTY-TWO

"Teach Without Teaching"

From the very beginning you must give your prospects the appearance of "how to" without teaching them a single thing. **You do this by making your prospects aware of the problem, and then convince them that you have the solution – but they'll have to pay you in order to get that solution.** Make them aware of some very interesting things that are connected to your solution, without actually giving them the solution until they pay for it. Promise them that you'll give them what they want. Because as Samuel Johnson said back in the 1700s, "A big promise is the soul of every great advertisement." Tell them what to do, and why they must do it, but never tell them how to do it.

Now, there's a time and a place when we definitely want to tell people everything. That's the purpose of seminars like the one upon which this book is based: to strip all the layers aside. Initially, however, you have to sneak up on people just a little before you lay the whole story out.

Of course, in some fields this tactic is something you absolutely want to avoid, since information needs to be passed forward so that things can be accomplished consistently, and in the case of the military and medical services, so that lives can be saved. **But, the free flow of information is not such a good thing if you're in business.** Depending upon your background, it may take you a while to realize this – but you have to make that switch if you expect to profit. You need to understand that when you're selling something to somebody, giving them all the

---

bare-bones information has nothing to do with selling. What you have to do is start out by providing the appearance of content.

One of the best sales pieces I ever got was a little yellow Jeff Paul book called *How to Make $4,000 In Your Underwear*. It's a great book because you pay nineteen bucks for it, and it's really a disguised pitch. It tells Jeff's story, and you really get into it, and then at the very end there's a little bit about how he started his information marketing business by focusing on niche markets. **You read the book, get excited and then ask yourself, "Great, how do I do it?"** <u>**And the information isn't there**</u>. To get it, you have to respond to Jeff's pitch.

Jeff Paul's book is a good model: **The idea is to give you a little taste, and spark an interest in you, so you say, "Yeah, this makes sense! It's really exciting!"** Then you try to figure it out on your own; but if you can't and finally give up and say, "Oh, heck, I'll just give Jeff his money," and send off for his course. That's where you get the real specifics.

In fact, that's how John Alanis built the basics of his system. But he didn't get to that without going through the appearance of content in the sales pitch, then buying it to get all the content there. <u>What this illustrates is that when you're selling, you have to do the things that sell. That has nothing to do with transmission of information; it has to do with selling</u>. You're educating people on all the reasons why they need what you sell. And so to do that, you're telling them why it's so important. In the beginning you're not giving them any secrets; if they want the secrets, they've gotta pay for them.

What you're trying to do is just offer reasons why they need what it is that you sell. You're creating that vacuum for what you have to offer, and you're teasing and taunting them just a little bit in order to get them to give their money to you.

Irritation Forms Pearls

Here's a very simple strategy that's directly related to every single sale that we make in our own market. **When a prospect raises their hand – that is, when they've responded to whatever lead generation you've put before them – in the next sales piece, consider trying to aggravate them.** Identify a problem for them. In John Alanis' case, one of the customer's biggest problems is feelings of inadequacy. If John wanted to aggravate them, he could take that problem and make a big deal of it. He could just say, "Okay, I have a program that would help you with that," but it's more profitable to open up that scab of inadequacy and pour salt in the wound. **That may sound horrible, but it's the way effective selling works.** You want to pile it on and pile it on before you offer that solution.

People will do so much to avoid pain, which is why this technique works. A lot of what we do as marketers starts with identifying a problem that our best prospective buyers have – whether it's that they don't have enough money, or they can't get women, or they're suffering the heartbreak of psoriasis. **We identify that problem, we make sure that we thoroughly understand the problem they have, and then we have to agitate that problem**. This has less to do with sharing information than it does with salesmanship and setting them up for the sale.

So once we've identified the problem, we pull back that scab and we pour salt on it. **We make them feel that pain. We figuratively put the knife in and, yes, twist it to make them feel worse.** Now that the pain's at its maximum, <u>what's the only solution that we've developed in their mind?</u> **Buying our product**. Giving us their money. That's the only way they're going to avoid this pain. This is a powerful technique, and it works all the time in so many different markets, whether you're selling antiperspirant or houses.

But it's one of the big principles of advertising and marketing that most business people aren't using, because they're not ruthless enough. They think that in causing their customers pain, they're going to drive them away. **But in the end, this technique sets your customers up to say, "Here's my money. I need what you're offering."** That's not to say that figuratively twisting the knife isn't going to drive some customers away; it will. But that should be okay; you've got to get past all of that. <u>You can't please everybody</u>. You have to be willing to offend some people and you must be willing to put it all on the line, or you'll never make the big profits that could and should be yours.

Changing Their Minds,
a Spoonful at a Time

I'll admit that the whole idea of appearing to pass information on to people without actually doing so – and in fact, tweaking their pain in the process – is ruthless. Well, that's why you're reading this, right? **This is a powerful marketing principle, and ultimately you're not misleading people; you're just not telling them everything.** You can't just give it all to people right away; you have to spoon-feed things to them a little bit at a time, and that's part of why we go through this process of the appearance of "how to" without the actual "how to."

If they want to know all the answers, they've got to go through the toll position that you've created in order to get them. Besides, you can't give people all the answers right away anyway – because you'll just overwhelm them and freak them out, and they'll run away.

The important point, again, is to keep in mind the difference between pre-sale and post-sale. Obviously, if you're delivering information products, after the sale you want to be all about the "how to." You want to tell them everything – because they've paid for it, and now you've got to deliver. Once you're aware of this technique, you'll see it in use everywhere, particularly in platform sales.

When you go to an event and see someone on stage whose end goal is to sell you their information product, you get a very clear example of the appearance of "how to." Most of them **use PowerPoint to show you their pitches these days. They've got slides running, and they're giving you all kinds of content…but not really.** It just appears that way. You feel like you're learning stuff, and you're sitting there taking lots of notes, and then all of a sudden they start their close – and it's not until then that you realize you really don't know anything at all, except (if they do it right) why you need whatever it is they're selling.

Everything that they've been doing up until that point has been about giving you reasons why you need their product. They're telling you a little bit, but not much. **Basically, the only reason they're telling you anything is so you know what you need to know – so that when it comes time to close, you know that they can give you more of what you think you already got from them (but really didn't).** All they're doing is educating you on why you need their particular product or service, and that's fine. That's where the "how to" comes in.

It's almost like a game of romance. If we only knew going into the game all the things we'd have to do, the prices we'd have to pay for everything that we're trying to achieve – whether it's a happy married life, or whether it's millions of dollars in the bank – we might not pay it. **That's why I talk about spoon-feeding people, showing them a little bit of the benefits at a time.** The allure of what it is that they want, whether it's six-pack abs or six million dollars in the bank, becomes the romance that leads them on to the true education of what it takes to get what they want.

Take the way excersise equipment is sold on TV. They don't focus too much on the diet and exercise part of it. **They tell you, "Just sit down with this machine for 10 minutes a day, and you'll look like this guy or this one."** But that can't happen – not without everything that goes with it. <u>They're giving you some information without the real information, and hoping you won't recognize that</u>. In a similar vein, one of the popular diet messages is, "Eat all the foods you want and still lose weight." Everybody knows better, but the promise is so big they want to believe it. Everybody knows it's really not true – at least without a lot of exercise and a special diet; but they all want to believe it.

There's an exercise machine advertised in every issue of Forbes that promises you can get in great shape from exercising four minutes a day, as long as you're willing to pay, oh, $15,000 for the machine. It's in every issue. And everybody knows that's BS, but they want to believe it, because it just might be true this time. **People want to believe.** You see all the diet ads, and they always have the pictures of the cakes and the cookies and all these fattening foods, and then they have the headline, "Eat all you want and still lose weight." **Does that mean that it's totally misleading? Well, probably a lot of it is.** Certainly Nutri-System has their little cake and cookies that supposedly won't make you fat if you don't eat too many of them – but you're not supposed to eat 16 of them.

If this principal bothers you, if you think it's just too ruthless, consider this: in a perfect world, you could just tell people everything right up-front and they would buy. **But in our imperfect world, you must lead people on; you have to offer them a little romance!**

CHAPTER TWENTY-THREE

"Demand Their Money!"

A marketing principle I try to live by is this: don't ask the people reading your sales material for their order. **Demand that they give you their money!** Make them feel bad if they don't. <u>This is what separates the big dogs from the whimpering puppies in the marketing field</u>.

In your Call to Action, whatever that may be – whether you're asking for $5,000 or $50,000 – you can't be passive-aggressive about it. **You've got to take them by the hand, you've got to lead them right where you want them to go, you've got to pick up the pen, you've got to put it in their hand, and you've got to get them to write that check or to sign that credit card authorization.** That's the bottom line, and you can't be passive about it. By that point, you need to have already built a good, strong case with the features and the benefits and the reasons why they should buy.

Going back to the PAS example I mentioned in Chapter 22, you've peeled that scab back, you've poured salt in it, you've made them feel the pain, and now the only solution is that they must buy whatever it is you're selling. At that point you can't be wimpy about it. **You're asking them for money, and you must be very bold.** As I like to say, **"<u>Timid salespeople raise skinny kids</u>."**

Which bring us to your Order Form. This is a very important part of the sales piece, because it's where you're reiterating those main features and benefits and reasons why they need your product or service. Boom – here it is, fill it out, mail it in, fax it in, let's do it! Let's act now! It also helps to have a little bit of urgency built in. **Whether it's contrived urgency or not, there's got to be a deadline to act now because it will increase your conversions**. You have to demand that they act immediately.

This is a secret I got from Ted Thomas, one of the top five platform speakers in the world. **Every salesperson knows they're supposed to ask for the order; that's in every marketing book there is**. But Ted Thomas says that one of the secrets of his success is that he doesn't just ask for the order, he demands the order – after he's done a thorough job of delivering his presentation, of course. And does he make enemies? Yes. Do a bunch of people not like him? Yes. **But does he get results? Hell yes**.

Robert Cialdini covers this very important concept, which is something that a lot of people really don't talk about, in his book *Influence: The Psychology of Persuasion*. He talks about all the different forms of persuasion: reciprocity and commitment, consistency, liking and others. **One that he includes is authority**. I don't think people talk about authority enough, at least from a business perspective.

In my business, one thing that I've made sure to do is build my business around an attractive character who has a strong sense of authority, because people gravitate towards people in authority. **When it comes to asking for the order, whether it's in a platform selling environment or whether it's in a sales letter, you have to ask for it with authority – because if you do it from a meek, mild, wimpy point of view, people feel uncomfortable.** They feel nervous. They feel like maybe you're pulling something, and so they don't buy.

When you ask for their order with a firm sense of

The Ruthless Marketing Attack!

conviction and a firm sense of authority – what I would call likeable authority – people feel very comfortable and very good about giving you their money. They think, "Okay, here's a person who's going to stand up, act like a leader, take responsibility, and make it acceptable for me to order."

If somebody is looking to you for a solution, they're conferring authority on you. If you're selling something to somebody, they perceive you as an expert, and they expect you to act in a particular way – with a sense of authority. **If you don't act like an authority, as they expect you to, they're not going to order, because they feel nervous.** So it's very important that you act the way they expect you to act. If you don't, that will kill the sale. **No matter the sales venue, if you ask for that item in a meek, mild, wimpy manner, you're not going to get it.**

Consider this. Did you guys know that you can tell your doctor "no" when they try to write you a prescription? **But how often does that happen?** Rarely, because they have the authority to make you believe that's what you need (and usually, or course, it is). Most of us just take the paper right to the pharmacist and have them fill the order. It's because doctors just tell you how it's going to be. They demand you submit to their authority. **When a doctor tells you that you need to do something, you generally do it. That comes from their position as authority in the field of medicine.**

Well, it's the same way with your product or service. **You're the authority, the expert, on that product**. You understand it better than any client could; you know it inside out and know it works. That's what they want to hear: your confidence, your sense of authority. **If you believe in your product, if you believe it's going to provide the promised benefits to your client, then with all your being you should be trying to convince them to place their order now.** If you're shy about asking for the order, then that shows them you don't have any confidence in your product – so why should they? I think that's the key to being authoritative in a way that sells products; it's in having the belief that your product really is worth the money you're asking them to give you…and that you really do believe that they'd be foolish not to get out their wallet right now and order. **If you have that belief, then you can convey that belief to them with confidence.** If you seem reserved or shy, they're going to instantly believe something is up. They're thinking, "Why are you being timid in asking for my money? What's wrong with your product, that you don't even believe in it enough to be confident in telling me I need it?" **Jay Abraham, arguably one of the best marketing experts around, says that <u>people are silently begging to be led.</u>** And I know that you'll probably agree with that, except for when it comes to you!

So once you've made your case, confidently (but politely) demand that they buy. Don't overdo it – just speak your piece, make your argument, and ask them to okay the order. Specific language can be very important: for example, instead of saying "How do you want to pay for this?" it may be more effective to say, "Would you prefer to take care of your investment via Visa or MasterCard?" These are two different approaches that can make a huge difference in selling. **This doesn't just work well in face-to-face selling situations; it translates over to ads, sales letters, web sites, etc; it translates over to how you present yourself; it translates over to everything.** <u>Precision of language and an attitude of total authority is a very powerful thing</u>. You've got to use it to lead your prospects right to the sale. When you come right down to it, leadership is all about persuasion and salesmanship.

CHAPTER TWENTY-FOUR

"The Benefit is What's Really Important"

I'm going to let you in on a big secret that should underlie everything you do as a marketer: the customer does not want your products and services. That's not why they buy them. **They only want what they perceive as the end result, the benefit they think they'll get when they give you their money.** Most business people never figure this out. This makes life so much easier for those of us who have.

What I've just said may seem counterintuitive. You may be thinking, **"What do you mean my customers don't want my products and services? Why else are they buying?"** Well, that's a good question, isn't it? But think about it. **Whatever people buy, they buy for the perceived benefit it will bring them – whether that's warmth, speed, money, or social prestige.** So really, making any money through marketing ultimately goes back to building a case in their minds that lets them fully perceive the benefits they'll receive from buying a product, service, or opportunity from you. This is directly applicable to many different businesses: people buy perceived value. **You're not necessarily selling that product, service, or opportunity.** You're trying to build a case in their mind of what they're going to get. The picture you're ultimately trying to paint is that if they buy this, their problem will be solved.

Most business people don't really see that. They think they're selling cheeseburgers, but maybe they should be selling fun. Look at Subway sandwiches; to continue the food analogy, that's a perfect example. Subway revolutionized their entire business when they started selling not sandwiches, but a healthy alternative to cheeseburgers. **People don't necessarily want sandwiches; they want their hunger to be fulfilled in a healthy yet tasty way.** In marketing, they teach us that people don't want quarter-inch drill bits; what they want is quarter-inch holes. They go out and buy the quarter-inch bit so they can get their quarter-inch holes – but what if there was an alternative to getting quarter-inch holes? What if you could shine a laser at the wood and drill those holes in a split-second, or dribble a liquid on the wood that drilled that hole? Would those sell? Of course they would, as long as they were reasonably safe. **Many people would completely forgo buying the drill bits, because the drill bits were only a means to an end.** What they really wanted were the holes.

Years ago, the marketing guru Ted Nicholas invented a copywriting strategy he called "The Hidden Benefit." Basically, what he said was, "If I had God-like super powers and could bestow upon my prospects anything that they wanted, what would it be?" That really forces you to think. His example was a book of corporate forms, and there's nothing more boring than that. But the headline he wrote about that was, "*What will you do when the I.R.S. seizes your personal assets to satisfy a judgment against your corporation?*" **Now, if you're a business owner and you read that, and you have the idea of the I.R.S. coming in, seizing your assets, and putting you in jail – well, you're going to read that thing!** The hidden benefit of it was that it taught you an important lesson: if you're ever taken to tax court about something, you have to keep proper corporate records, or you could pierce the corporate veil and they can come seize your personal assets. Ted's book of corporate forms keeps you from getting in trouble with the I.R.S.; **he scared the holy hell out of everybody with that, and sold $70 million worth.**

To understand the dichotomy between actual products

and benefits, you need look no further than what most information marketers sell – for example, this is true of myself, Chris Lakey, John Alanis and, to a lesser extent, Chris Hollinger. If an outsider were to say to me, "Hey, T.J., let's see the product that you sell," I'd have to show them a bunch of CDs and manuals, wouldn't I? Is that what people want? No. **I'll tell you what people want: <u>they want the answers to their problems</u>**.

In John Alanis' case, they want to know how to instantly and automatically attract all the women they want without facing rejection: they want those women to just line up outside the door so that they can say, "You, you, and you." Even more than that, they want to show these women off to their friends and make them jealous. They want to be envied and admired. They want relief from feelings of inadequacy. **It's a matter of tapping into those basic human emotions**. And John can bestow that upon them, if they're willing to take action. Instead of letting them think, "I've been rejected. There must be something wrong with me as a man," John tells them, "No, you just don't have the right skills to get women." And he can pass on those skills, for a price. **John's not just selling some discs and manuals; he's selling a solution to a problem**. When you really tap into these emotions and realize that's really what your product does, that's when you get into some very, very powerful sales copy.

John used to run an art business. He was in the business of selling steel art, and one of the most successful headlines he ever used was a knock-off from an old John Caples headline: "*How to get your cooking bragged about*." John surveyed his customers and asked them, "What's the biggest benefit of this art?" and they'd all talk about they'd get the thing, then hang it in their home. All their friends would come over, cluster around it, and "ooh" and "aah." So John's headline there was, "*Here's how to get your home bragged about*." **That's a good example of tapping into what people really want – in this case, that social admiration from putting a rusty piece of metal on the**

wall. That's the hidden benefit: again, the relief of inadequacy. They felt that their home wasn't adequate, and this was a way for them to make their home more than adequate and to show off to people. **It's the same reason why a guy goes and buys a Corvette.** When you get right down to it, he could drive a bicycle to get him from Point A to Point B, and probably end up in better physical shape than anyone out there. **The truth is, if we all bought what we needed, we'd all be driving Yugos and living in trailers.** But some men want to put a 25-year-old hot blonde in the car and drive in front of his old balding buddies and show off what a successful guy he is. That's why he's buying a Corvette! It's the same reason a lot of guys get into the information marketing business – so they can make lots of money they can show off to their buddies and the women in their lives.

If you ignore these basic human emotions and don't link them to your product, you'll never be nearly as effective as you might be. So use the old Ted Nicholas method: **What's the hidden want? What's the hidden benefit? If you were omnipotent, what's the one thing that your product could do, the biggest benefit it could give your customers?** Consider that, and you'll come up with all kinds of amazing ideas that you couldn't think of before!

In a related vein, one of the more enlightened principles sometimes taught to marketers is that you should try to make the object transparent when writing copy. **What that means is, no matter what you're selling, describe it in such a way that the customer can see through it to look at the benefits.** For example, somebody who buys a Bentley isn't buying the car for driving. They can do that in a Ford Focus or a Chevy Nova. Look past the car, and what you're getting is the benefit of prestige. People look at your car and say, "Wow, you can afford a Bentley." **So the more transparent the object, the better you can see the benefit through it**. Say you've got a big box of tapes, CDs, and manuals that make up, for example, the recorded version of the seminar upon which this book is based. You're not going to say, "Look here! This is a nice box, and it's got some of the best-looking CDs in it you'll ever have!" No, you're selling the "dream" or the "image" that the information here is going to give your customers. **You have to paint that rosy picture of what their life is going to be like once the customer has your product**. The salesman who sold that guy the Corvette I mentioned above probably painted a great picture: "You're really going to be able to pick up babes with this!"

The unspoken part of that is that he probably also painted the negative picture of what would happen if the bald guy didn't buy that little red Corvette. It all goes back to ratcheting up the pain, the practice of opening that scab and pouring in the salt that I talked about in Chapter 22. To go back to John Alanis again, what he does is say, "Look, you're at a crossroads in your life right now. You can either take action and get all these benefits, or you can be forever lonely. You can die alone and unloved and forgotten. So which do you want? " You've got twin forces, positive and negative, working for you. **Remember, in many cases people are more likely to act to avoid pain than to move toward pleasure.** So give them something to move towards, and something to move away from; make them feel bad about not buying and also feel good about buying. In other words, don't be afraid to use both the carrot and the stick to urge people to buy.

CHAPTER TWENTY-FIVE

"Deal Aggressively with Competition"

The opportunity market, the one in which I've been working since 1988, is loaded with competition. But I've developed an attitude where I don't worry unduly about the competition, and I think most true entrepreneurs are the same way. **How often do we really focus on our competitors?** Well, we take their sales material and put it in our swipe files, and we adapt their ideas sometimes, and sometimes use them as templates to come up with our own products. That's all part of ruthless marketing. But how much time do we really sit around worrying about them and all that nonsense? Not much. **For one thing, they're helping bring more people into our market, which means, in absolute numbers, there's more for us. For another, most of them aren't willing to use the ruthless strategies I discuss in this book, so I'm eventually going to capture some of their market share anyway.**

I actually like having successful competitors in my market space, because it gives me the opportunity to do profitable Joint Ventures with them. Besides, think of it this way: even if you're selling the same type of thing, a buyer is a buyer is a buyer. **A buyer is unlikely to purchase one product of a specific type; they're more likely to purchase them all, so even if he's buying from your competitor, it's quite likely he'll give you a try also.** There's a great old-time mail order marketer named Jim Straw, a fantastically smart guy, who is adamant about the fact there's no competition in this business; there are only contemporaries. All of the other great marketers in the

---

Direct Response Marketing business are investing huge sums of money to get customers, and if they're smart and don't have the scarcity mentality, then it's an opportunity for you to do endorsed Joint Ventures with them, because they've already spent the time and energy and effort and money to build the relationship. **So when you come along and do an endorsed mailing or something to their list, the response is phenomenal!** <u>If you think of other people in your business as cooperation, there's always an opportunity to make more money</u>. It's an environment full of cooperation, not competition.

Having said that, I have to point out that how well you can handle competition depends on the size of your market. For example, my best friend's pest control business is located in a mid-sized city, Wichita, where there's a lot of demand. As for us, we're working with people all over the nation; some of my colleagues, especially those who are Internet-based, have clients all over the world. But, if you're in a small market you may be in trouble. A friend of mine, Keith Banman, owns the local grocery store in Goessel. If another grocery store comes to town, one or the other will probably be going out of business within the year. This market, as it exists, isn't big enough to support two grocery stores. But the key term here is "as it exists." If Keith were able to change his mindset and retool his business, he might still survive. **One way to do this is to remember that the Internet is out there, and that changes your marketplace from local to global, if you want it to be. Look at the Harry & David Company, or Omaha Steaks**. They're selling grocery store commodities to the entire world; they have lists that they market to vigorously, and they're making tons of money.

On the other hand, if you're selling the same thing to the same group of people, the first thing you have to do is differentiate yourself with a Unique Selling Position, or USP. Tell them exactly why they should do business with you as opposed to doing business with anybody else or as opposed to doing nothing. **Then get that USP out there in the marketplace; tell them your story, build a relationship with your customers, send out a monthly newsletter or emails or something similar – and in so doing, put an iron cage around the customers, <u>moving the relationship away from the product that you're selling, to the personality behind the product</u>.** Get that story out there and bond with the customers. If you get that set up right, no one's going to be able to come in and easily take over what you've built, not even something like Wal-Mart or Alco, because people are doing business with people and the story – which transcends the product. <u>The fact is, the product is actually the least important part of the business</u>. You can get products anywhere.

What's really important is the relationship with your customers, and the personality behind it; that's the driving force that gets people to bond with you. **You develop a close relationship with the customer, so that when it comes time for them to buy a specific product, they'll give their money to you rather than one of your competitors.** You see, there's a big dose of politics in business, in addition to that combination of art, science, war, and sports. You have to get people to know you and trust you. As I was writing this book, I saw a news show on TV in which, every night, they interviewed a new politician running for president. One night, they interviewed a candidate whom I'd never heard of before. He had a great story to tell, and I thought, "Why don't more people know about this guy? Why don't I see him in the polls?" **As far as I was concerned, he was an unknown. <u>You can't let that happen to you in business or politics</u>.** In large part, both are about personality, and positioning. Now, that candidate has no shot of winning, but maybe he should; he's got a great story to tell, and yet hardly anyone knows it.

Even in a small town like Goessel, Kansas, you'd better believe that there's a lot of politics that go on here, for a variety of reasons. That would be one of the resources that an entrepreneur like our local grocer, Keith, would be able to tap into. In a situation in which someone new comes and tries to take over the business, my suggestion would be to go back to the 10 key Smart Marketing steps I discussed in Chapter 13, study them closely, and learn how to leverage them the best you can.

Realize that you're in a fight for the life of your business, and you need out-hustle them to survive. **Really address those Smart Marketing steps, and then make up your mind and be realistic with yourself.** Okay, so you've got some serious competition in your marketplace now; it's going to force you to either fail, or to improve – to change, to make yourself seem more unique, to find a niche where you can serve your customer better than any competition. Go that route and you're going to win that battle, but it's not going to come easy. You're going to have to do some serious thinking about your marketing, your positioning in your market, and how you're going to serve those customers better than the competition.

Serving your customers is crucial – because ultimately, competition is good for the consumer. As an example, let's take another look at Keith's Foods, the local grocery store. Thirty years ago it probably would have been an accurate statement to say that the Co-Op that preceded Keith's Foods had no competition. They were the only gig in town, and very few people who lived here went anywhere else. But today it's easy to drive 10 miles down the road to Wal-Mart or Dillon's in Newton, Kansas, the next closest community, to get your groceries, so at some level he's competing with them.

So Keith has to be smart about what he does, or else he's losing market share. **His ultimate goal would be to have every single person in this town of four or five hundred people buying all their groceries from him and nowhere else.** That's not going to happen, but that would be his ideal. If he does everything right, gains the maximum market share, ideally he'd even have people from other smaller communities around coming here to buy their stuff. **Right now that's not happening; he doesn't have that entire market share, so he's not doing everything he could be doing.** He's got competition, though not in this town directly – he's got people who choose to drive away to the next closest town where they can shop at Wal-Mart or Dillon's.

Of course we all feel a little guilty when we do that, those of us who know Keith… But here's a cool, true story. There I was at Wal-Mart doing my grocery shopping, and who do I run into? Keith from the local grocery store! He'd just had knee surgery so he's driving around in one of those little electric carts, and I started feeling really guilty – I know I should be doing more business with him, because he's a great man. And then all of a sudden I'm thinking, "Well, what the hell is Keith doing here?" **It turns out he buys all of his produce at Wal-Mart, because he can get local produce fresher and cheaper at Wal-Mart than he can from his own produce wholesaler!** That's kind of like what I talked about in Chapter 11 with the scrapbook store – only Keith is actually doing it. Here he is, shopping at Wal-Mart, so he can resell to his own customers.

But here's another thing he's doing: he has a catering business on the side that represents significant profits for him. He's involved in every single event possible within a 20-mile radius, and he serves up lunch at a lot of our events. **It's a sideline business, and he's doing all kinds of other stuff on the side, too; things he offers that nobody else does.** For example, on Friday afternoons – and sometimes twice a week – Keith grills hamburgers outside his store, and all the local people come. He's put in a fast-food pizza place in his store. He sells videos. He's got an old-fashioned deli that's like stepping back into the fifties, and he's got some really good deli sandwiches – his deli makes better sandwiches than those franchise joints. And his Lebanon bologna…well, he could sell that all across the country. All in all, he's got a nice little quaint small-town American store that comes with a lot of specialty items.

So Keith is competing, and he's doing so effectively. He's gotten beyond the boogeyman or thinking he has to compete with the next guy, instead he's being a good entrepreneur, looking at all the different things available, and creating the business he needs.

Keith has really increased the lifetime value of his customers, and he has all these different products and services. **It's not a product business he's got; it's a customer-driven business.** The way he thinks is, "I've got this customer, and I can sell them videos, and Lebanon bologna, and all this other stuff that other guys won't." So he's got a fantastic opportunity here. But at the same time, he could be doing so much more, and he does have the opportunity to do so.

He may be happy and doing really well with what he's got now, but if he really wanted, he could get in the information business and teach other people how to aggressively compete in their own small towns all across America. **He could go to all kinds of businesses in his related area – the struggling grocery stores who are struggling with the same problems that he is overcoming – and show them how to increase their profits**. He could do all kinds of workshops, tele-seminars, or offer them a big $30,000 a year coaching program – and in so doing, make ten times more money than he makes working in his own store.

The Real Competition

Here's something about competition that a lot of people don't think about: the competition is real, <u>but it's not</u>

really product-versus-product competition. What it's competition for is attention. There's competition for your mailbox space, your e-mail space, your television and radio airwaves. That's why you've got to P.T. Barnumize everything you do, about which I talked in Chapter 19. **You've got to make things big, bold, outrageous and audacious, because you're competing for people's attention.** It's not so much competition of one businessperson against another, because there's so much opportunity and so much money out there. **Because the amount of media has just absolutely exploded in the past 30 or so years, people have things coming at them from all directions, so they're going to be able to pay attention to only a portion of it** – and usually that's the part that's bright and flashy, that reaches out and grabs their attention. Everything else fades into the background.

At my company, M.O.R.E., Incorporated, we're not as Internet-based as some people out there, but folks like John Alanis and Chris Hollinger tell me that their big competition is spam email. For example, John does two emails a day, so he's got to find a way to get that email delivered, opened, and read in the face of a deluge of unwanted mail. **His competition is everything else that's happening on the Internet.** Plus, when his prospects check their email, is the dog barking, the kid screaming, the sexy girl they've been waiting to come online finally sending them an instant message? John – and anyone working on the Internet – has to compete for attention on more than a product-versus-product basis.

That's one of the reasons why good marketers constantly follow-up with people, constantly stay in touch with them – because you never know for sure when one of your communications is just going to fail to get through for a wide variety of reasons. We've all had days when we're so busy that all we do is go through all of our emails as fast as we can, just to see how many we can delete in the quickest period of time. You don't want to read any of them, because you're so overwhelmed and you're under all this pressure. So you might miss something you would ordinarily have taken the time to read and act upon, on any other day. **The point is, you never know when you're going to catch a prospect at just the right time.** And face it, even if the prospect looks at every one of your emails (or direct mailings, or magazine ads, or however you're marketing), it might be a long time before they decide to buy.

This is especially the case with John Alanis, who sells products that teach you how to attract women. **He has guys who got on his email list <u>a year</u> before they bought**. They were curious when they got on; they just wanted to see what this crazy guy John had to say, then all of a sudden something happens – their new buddy meets a girl they're showing off, or their wife leaves them, or something else unexpected occurs. John had one guy who'd been on his list for 18 months, when he met this 26-year-old woman on the train to Moscow. They were going to spend two weeks together, but he didn't know what to do. So as soon as he got back, he bought everything John had to offer!

In the opportunity market I serve, around New Year's is often a great time, because the brother-in-law shows up and he's doing real well, and the guy who's going to buy feels bad. So he says to himself, "I'm going to make money this year," and he goes out and buys an opportunity product. **Since you never know when something's going to happen and you're going to be able to break through this constant barrage of attention-grabbing clutter and various life-events, <u>if you're not in front of them constantly, you're not going to get through to them</u>**. That's why this multi-step, multi-media method is more important than ever, and why you have to leverage the power of hype to get their attention.

Let me read you one of John Alanis' ads, which is

featured in a great book by some friends of mine called the *Official Get Rich Guide To Information Marketing* (ISBN-10-159918140-1). There's a feature story about John Alanis, and they've got his full-page advertisement on page 77. I want to include it here, because this is what I would call using the power of hype in your market. I'm going to describe it rather than print it, because for my purposes the message, I think, is more important than his graphics.

He starts out with, "Do you hate rejection by women?" (This is the pre-head.) "Imagine no more heartbreak, no more rejection, ever…." He's got a picture of a beautiful young lady right there on the side, which is a nice attention-grabber for people flipping through the pages. And then here's the headline in rather big type. It says, "The amazing natural attraction secrets of a 5' 7" former loser from Texas that literally compels beautiful, desirable women to approach you first, begging you for a date no matter what your looks are, or your age or your income." **That's just brilliant!**

And then he's got another sub-head that says, "WARNING: When you put these women-approach-you secrets to work, you must be careful not to attract too many women too fast. Why would any sane man reveal these secrets in a FREE Report if they were true? Read my amazing message to find out." **This is brilliant stuff. I can't imagine any guy who's struggling with this issue who wouldn't read this full-page advertisement.**

Hype is different for every market, but that's the best example in John's market. **This is what gets people's attention**. It cuts through the clutter. That's where you really have to focus on competition. **You have to realize how apathetic people are these days, how inundated they are with other advertising and marketing messages, how immune they've become**. If there's one good justification for hype, it's that you can break free of the clutter and jump off that radar screen and grab their attention.

By the way, the warning about being careful not to attract too many women may seem a little familiar – it's been used by other markets in a similar ways. John tells me he got it from a weight-loss ad that had a disclaimer that said, "WARNING: When you take this product, you must be careful not to lose too much weight too fast." Certain male enhancement ads do something similar when they warn you about the possibility of the drug working too well – we've all heard the warning about seeing a doctor if an erection lasts for more than four hours, right?

And John got the "Why would any sane man reveal this…" from an old Jeff Paul ad. **In other words, he swiped some good ideas and modified them for his own use, and they worked**. It's that whole psychology of, "if they're warning me against that huge benefit that I'm looking for, then even if I don't get that result, if I get close to that result, I'm doing good!

If it's possible to lose too much weight too fast, then maybe even if I lose just a little bit of weight, I'll still be happy with the results." By the way, there's a warning on that weight loss ad that says something like, "This is not for people who just want to lose a little weight; this is for people who want to lose 30 pounds, 40 pounds, or a hundred pounds!" **Of course, the thought process is, "Wow, if it works for them, what's it going to do for me?"** That's what John Alanis' ad does. Notice the imagery the ad generates in your head. Imagine some guy who wants to meet women. You need to try to crawl into his head and determine what's going to get this guy's attention. Well, John's headline is a "stop-it" for any guy in that market. When he sees it, he's going to think, "Heck yeah, what's this all about?" **It's going to grab his attention because it has that emotional appeal to it – and it works because John knows his market,**

and those words speak to them. I'll tell you something very interesting about that ad, too. The "imagine no more heartbreak, no more rejection ever" line came from a series of dating emails that John tested, and for whatever reason, that subject line always got a much better response. It resonated. So when he went back to writing full-page ads, he took all the appeals that had worked via email and put them in there. **That's actually where his marketing copy came from: scientific testing, not just from being a good copywriter.** Every appeal in that ad is something that was tested beforehand via email, which cut down on the risk when John ran that particular advertisement. That's especially important, because if something is catchy enough to stand above the crowd in email, where normally people will hit delete if it doesn't grab them in the first few sentences, then it's likely to work in just about any medium.

Speaking of the Crowd...

I've spoken about how competition is good in many ways, as long as you don't let it scare you. In fact, the last thing you want to do is get involved in a market where there's not a lot of thriving competitors. **You must look for marketplaces where lots of people are already thriving, because that tells you that there is, in fact, a market for what you're selling**. A lot of people make the biggest mistake in their business when they select the wrong market in which to work. If you try to sell something to people who aren't buying, well, of course you're going to have a difficult time. **So when you're doing your initial marketing research, you need to find a market with a lot of competition. But note this – <u>it doesn't have to be good competition</u>!**

The one thing that you have to do in order to be a ruthless marketer is to find a way to stand out. Just like a good politician on the campaign trail who really wants that public office, you've got to find a way to stand head and shoulders above all of the other competitors, to show that you're the best, that you're the one to whom they should give their money. John Alanis tells me that when he did his initial market research, he went to Google and typed in "dating" and similar items to see what would come up. He found a lot of stuff, and he knew it had to be working, since it was based on pay-per-click ads they were paying for every single day. **If it didn't work, people wouldn't have paid for it, and some of these sites were up constantly for weeks, so it was obvious they had to be making money**.

But the plain truth was, their marketing was terrible! That's when John knew he could kick butt in that marketplace. You see, the market was so hungry that even bad marketing could make money. **When you introduce good marketing to those starving people, they respond in droves, and you're going to clean up.** So that's what you want to look for. Is there a marketplace where people are prospering with bad marketing? Because if there is, it's a tremendous opportunity.

Now remember, let's take that one step backwards to what I've talked about earlier in this book. This is not intended as a judgment call; this just happens to be an observation. **Most business people – especially in the local brick-and-mortar sector – are lousy marketers.** That should serve as a great confidence booster for anybody who wants to rise above that and accomplish something. In Chapter 1, I discussed the fact that in the land of the blind, the one-eyed man is king. **You don't have to be that much better that everyone else to kick butt in the marketplace – which should be obvious, since so many people are doing such a lousy job, and they're still making their businesses work.** You know that you can come along and just tweak what they're doing and add some ideas from some of these other sharp marketers – even in other fields – and you'll have an almost unfair advantage over all of your competitors.

The Ruthless Marketing Attack!

CHAPTER TWENTY-SIX

"Love Thine Enemies"

One ruthless marketing tip that I always provide my seminar attendees is, "Thank God for my enemies. They spur me on. They give me a reason to fight." **For me, that's an important motivation; people are motivated for different reasons, but anger and irritation can be a good one.** Chris Hollinger tells me that when he was competing at basketball in college, he honestly played better if he was absolutely pissed off at the other team. Sometimes he'd have to sit there and stare at them before the game, and invent reasons to be mad at them! Oftentimes, he was friends with the guys on the other team – but not while he was playing. **In other words, he built up his energy, so to speak, with anger.** Sometimes he used every ounce of creativity he had just to come up with a reason to be angry, because he played better if he was angry!

Well, the same thing happens in business, especially in a competitive environment. We've all seen competitive business people out there, and some of them can be cutthroat. **Some of them get wrapped up in the game, and they can say and do things they normally wouldn't; but in the heat of the moment they will, because their business and their livelihood depends on it**. They use that energy and that force and that competitive nature that goes all the way back to the Neanderthals, which can be very effective in business. <u>Think of how boring it would be if you were in a market that didn't have competition</u>. Look at it from a sports perspective – what kind of game would it be if you didn't have a competitor? In the NFL, for example, there's nothing better than a Division game where you have two rival teams playing. Sports is just drama in motion, and people are drawn to that drama. Similarly, business can be very dramatic, very competitive.

Here's a little story about these enemies, straight from Chris Hollinger, and it goes back to basketball. Lately he's been trying to get back into shape, so he's been playing with a group of his friends that all started in Bitty Basketball together, back when they were little kids. Many of them went to college, and sometimes they competed against each other there.

Nowadays they're all in their late 30s and early 40s – middle-aged men – and they play in a men's league out in El Dorado, Kansas, which they've won time and time again. Well, this past year they were warming up, and this younger team came in; not a single person on their team was over 25. **They didn't know Chris's and team and didn't realize that they'd been playing together a long time and had a high level of skill.**

Then one of them made the mistake of letting one of Chris' teammates hear them say, "These guys are old. We're going to ruin them." Well, that got back to the rest of the team, and within the first two minutes of the game, those young guys knew they weren't going to win. They knew they were in for a fight, because that statement pumped Chris Hollinger's team up even more. **They pissed them off, and they saw blood**. So by half-time the youngsters were down by over 30 points – and at the end of the game, the score was 96-60. The young guys just walked off the court with their heads down, and it was partly their own fault, because they made some enemies that night they didn't really need, and it got them slaughtered.

I think that's a good example of how you absolutely have to motivate yourself in business. **One thing I think is absolutely ridiculous is the way that local business owners often treat each other, especially in small towns**. They're all members of the Chamber of Commerce, they're all trying to get along with each other, they all try to do coffee together, and they have this "we're all in the same boat" mentality – like they're all supposed to be buddies. I think most of that is wrong.

It's great to Joint Venture with some of your competitors, sure, but in most marketplaces, your competitors are not your friends. Far from it. In earlier chapters I've mentioned my best friend, who has a pest control business in Wichita. She has a hundred other competitors, and most of those competitors are guys with single trucks who broke away from the companies for which they used to work. **Now, they have basically no overhead, which is definitely a competitive advantage over her when it comes to pricing the jobs; she has 15 trucks on the road, so she has a tremendous amount of overhead**. And every one of her employees looks at their competitors as the enemy; they're out there to kick their competitors' collective ass every single day of every single week! They don't practice this friendly little kind of "Hey, we're all in this together" competition. They're out there to kick butt, and they've got to have that attitude in order to overcome their disadvantages.

I see so many local business people with this whole attitude of, "We're all friends," and that's a big load of crap. **You can't be friends with your direct competitors.** Go out there and kick their butts! Look for ways to beat them. Look for ways that you can have competitive advantages over them.
I do think this can be carried too far, especially in some industries, but that spirit of camaraderie is something you have to avoid if you want to make the real money.

This is especially true in the Multi-Level Marketing world. If there was ever a cutthroat industry, it's MLM. And yet you have all these MLM distributors working for companies that act like we're all supposed to hold hands and sing songs. Bull! **These people are not your friends!** When it comes to business, they are your enemies. Quit holding hands with them! Get out of that mindset, or that boat you're all supposed to be in together is going to sink. **Worse, you may find out that those so-called buddies of yours have been stabbing you in the back the whole time you've been sharing tea and sympathy with them.** Either way – you're out of business or they're taking away sales and profits that should have been yours.

So avoid playing nicey-nicey with your competitors, and avoid hiring employees who want to do that. **You don't want to think of your direct competitors as friends in any way, shape, or form, especially in smaller, more competitive marketplaces.**

If I were located in a small town and had a clothing store, and right across the street from me was another clothing store, I'd want to look for as many ways as possible to differentiate myself from them, and give my customers things that the other store didn't. **Every day that I showed up and put my "Open" sign up in my window, my goal for the day would be to put that guy across the street out of business as fast as I could.** I don't mean I'd do anything illegal or immoral, but I'd find as many ways to legally take away the other store's business as I could. That's because they're the enemy.

That doesn't mean that you necessarily hate them. As I'm writing this, there's a college football game coming up between the two big state schools in Kansas. **They've been talking on the news about it all week – about how both schools have been very cautious about saying anything that could tick the other team off, or stuff they could use as bulletin board material to fire up their team.** Well, the reason they're doing that is because they want to make sure the other team doesn't have any better reason to win, other than just trying to win.

It's really about the teams executing as best as they can. In a situation like this, whichever team wins is going to win, not because they're worried about what the other team is doing; it's because they're executing their game plan as well as they can. **So doing well in business is not really about the people who make up the competition.** Trying to beat them is less about them and more about you, and you executing your game plan and doing the best that you can in business. I'm not talking about hurting anybody; <u>I'm talking about playing a better game</u>.

We all want to be the best, and that's as it should be. No matter how much you like your competitors, even the ones you're willing to do Joint Ventures with, you have to keep this in mind: <u>there's only one company that can be the best</u>. That's where you want to be. **So at best, you're taking part in a friendly competition with some tension there, to find out who can sell the most, who can build the biggest business, who's the biggest expert, and then who can stay on top.** Once you get on top, somebody's going to try to knock you down – so you have to be very good to stay on top. And if you get knocked down, you want to get back up immediately. That's the healthy way to look at it. **At the very least, look at competitors and contemporaries as people you want to best, so that you can be King of the Hill. There's only that one slot at the top.** And if you have to, then motivate yourself with enemies. Most of us have people we don't like. You can find a way to use the way you feel about these people to your advantage.

Here's another point that connects with what I've already said in this chapter: you have to maintain a confident attitude in business. **Being confident isn't a matter of putting other people down so much as it is a feeling that you're superior at some level.** So I'm confident when dealing with my own 'enemies,' because I've forgotten more marketing knowledge than they've ever learned. That's how I set out to beat them.

Here's a story I particularly like that illustrates that doctrine of confidence very well. It's from Chapter 6 of John F.

Love's book, *McDonald's: Behind the Arches*. When McDonald's was just getting big in the emerging fast-food business in the late 1960s, there was a company around called Burger Chef, which is out of business now.

Very few people remember them, I suspect, even though they lasted until 1996. So here's an established Burger Chef, and a McDonald's opens up across the street. One day, the owner of the Burger Chef sees the McDonald's supervisor coming across the street, and he figures the guy wants to shake hands and introduce himself, and say something like, "Hey, if I ever run out of hamburger buns can I come over and get some, or maybe lend you some pickles when you're out? Because after all, they're all in this together, right?"

Well…not exactly.

The McDonald's area supervisor comes over to his shop to shake the Burger Chef owner's hand and introduces himself, sure enough, and the first thing he says after he introduces himself is, "We're going to put you out of business." Was that cocky? Absolutely. Was it rude? Maybe. **But it was also enormously confident, and I just love that attitude!** The first thing he said to the Burger Chef man was, "We're going to put you out of business." And eventually, they did!

Now, that's not Chamber of Commerce. When you get right down to it, as one of my seminar attendees once pointed out, **"That's destroying somebody else just so you can gain a nickel or two."** Well, duh: that's the name of the game. It's not nice, but it's true. <u>Only the fittest individuals survive in the animal kingdom, and the same is true in business</u>.

Consider this: the Burger Chef guy, and in fact the whole chain, didn't have to let themselves be put out of business. They had an opportunity to fight and put those upstarts at McDonald's out of business instead. **At the very least, they might have put up enough of a fight to keep both businesses strong just from fighting each other off and being at odds all the time.** That's how survival of the fittest works. At some level, if you've succumbed to another business, either you were incapable of surviving a fight, or you chose to succumb to it. You decided not to fight hard enough.

To those people who think that most of what's wrong with this country is because of this conflict between businesses, I have to respectfully disagree. **I feel that competition is the greatest thing in the world. It only serves the consumer in the end, because it gives people more choices than they ever had before on a variety of products and services that might not have existed without competition.**

My father, God rest his soul, was a great man. But one of the things that he and I used to argue about furiously was the fact that the government broke up AT&T – and now there were all these competitors, so he couldn't get good service. I used to say, "Dad, that's nonsense," and we'd have violent arguments about it, to the point where he was shouting at me, and I was shouting at him. I felt then (and still do) that the breakup of AT&T generated all kinds of competition that ultimately created amazing thing; cellular phones, for example.

In Chapter 11, I told you the story of the Ben Franklin store in Hillsboro, Kansas. They found out that Alco was coming to town, and they immediately put up their "Going Out of Business" sign. **They didn't even try to stay in business.** Even now, I'm dumbfounded by that reaction. I mean, come on! **This is a competitive environment, and ruthless marketing is all about competing**. And, yes, ultimately, it's the consumer that ends up with more choices and better prices. New products and services are developed, niche markets start breaking into smaller niche markets, and smaller niche markets start breaking into even more. If companies hadn't kept competing head-to-head and evolving that way, would we have mobile phones? Would we have computers? How about cheap air conditioning, grocery store scanners, televisions, electrical dishwashers, or any of those other things that make life easier or more enjoyable? Probably not. **In the end, entrepreneurs who were willing to duke it out in the marketplace made all this happen.**

While there may be some destructive elements in all this, the fact is that free markets are what drive the economy. Even long-time socialist and communist countries are finally admitting this. Now, when I say, "Thank God for my enemies," the statement with which I started this chapter, once again I'm using more extreme language than others might. **Just as I choose to use the term "ruthless marketing" instead of "aggressive marketing" or "assertive marketing," I'm using the term "enemies" rather than "competitors."** I do this to drive home the point, because it's ruthless (aggressive, assertive) competition that drives businesses, business owners and entrepreneurs to be better. Competition in the free market drives innovation.

Here's a small example: the iPod. Before it came out, MP3 music players were crappy little expensive things that could maybe hold ten or twenty songs – and that was it. Then Apple Computers – under Steve Jobs again – looked at the problem and said, "Why can't we use a high-density computer drive to store music?" And so out comes the iPod, which was a little bigger and heavier than most MP3 players, and yes, a little more expensive – but it could store literally thousands of songs. Not tens or hundreds, thousands. **And did that spur Rio and the other companies to make better MP3 players? You're damn right it did!** It was either that or go out of business, which some did.

On a smaller scale, competition drives entrepreneurs to be more successful, to be better at their business – which makes their competitors want to be better at their business, makes the markets respond, and makes customers happier because it's all product and service-driven.

Without a common goal of being profitable, there's no innovation in the marketplace. **That means without enemies, without competition, you get stagnation in the marketplace.** Everything drops to the lowest common denominator, there's no innovation, and there's no drive to profitability that ends up helping the consumer. **If everything works out well, you get a Socialist economy where everybody is equally worthless – and so are the products available.** You're likely to get situations like you used to see in China and the Soviet Union, where the people at the top made sure they get all the good stuff, and everyone else has to stand in line for hours to get bread.

If there was no competition, there would be no reason to try to be better at your business, which ends up hurting consumers. **Every business exists to serve its customers and make a profit.** If you're not serving your customer and providing them with good value, you're not going to be profitable. The two go hand in hand. So the competition – the enemy – spurs you on to be a better entrepreneur, to serve your marketplace better.

Now, here's a cautionary note: as much as I talk about business being like war, keep in mind that in the world of business, when I talk about "killing" our competition, or when I talk about "destroying" our competitors, I'm not talking about physically laying a hand on them or engaging in any kind of skullduggery. I'm talking about a battle in the marketplace. **The worst thing that happens is that companies are financially destroyed, and their employees have to go out and find new jobs.** While this can be personally devastating, it's not the end of their lives. In fact, it can have a positive effect. **I got my butt kicked in business many times and I'm a much better man**

for it, believe me! I believe most of my colleagues can say that – and I know it's true for the entrepreneurs.

Creating a Common Enemy

Another interesting way to look at the concept of the enemy in business is to understand the concept of the common enemy. **Some people may not like it, but one of the most powerful ways you can do this in your marketing is to divide the world into "us" versus "them" – <u>no matter who your "them" is</u>.** If a common enemy doesn't exist, then you need to create one.

When you're building a customer list, your prospects will respond better when there's a common enemy against which to unite. You want it to be "me and you against the enemy." If you have to, you can manufacture that enmity.

In John Alanis' business, there's not really a common enemy; he's teaching men how to attract women. Though here's one that might work for him: the Tom Sellecks of the world, all the gifted men who were born to be on the cover of GQ Magazine – the guys who have all the advantages physically, and often monetarily. John calls them the jerks, the guys who swagger around in the locker rooms and that kind of thing. **But otherwise, he's created his own enemy by emphasizing the enmity between what he calls "talkers" and "doers." The enemy's the talker, while the good guy, <u>the guy that buys his product, is the doer.</u>** Talkers are the guys who don't behave the way he wants, and doers are the ones who do. If you want to be on John's good side…well, then, you're a doer. And it's John and his doers against all those talkers out there.

When you create these winners and whiners within your business, it has a polarizing and a bonding effect. It's one of those things that enhances your customer group. **Everyone has a common enemy**. If you can find the common enemy and bond with your customer group and set up an "us against them" mentality, then that will dramatically increase your sales. **It's a plain fact that sometimes, the best way to make a friend is to find out who your common enemies are.** That's how people bond.

Battles You Don't Need to Fight

While I'm all for ruthless competition, as you'll notice if you've read the last few chapters, there are some competitors that you don't necessarily have to worry about trying to beat. In some ways, you can work with them; you can do Joint Ventures with them, for example. This is especially true with all of your indirect competitors. **One thing you should always do is distinguish between your direct and indirect competitors.** There are people who are serving the same type of customers you want to serve who aren't competing directly with you. Those people should always be thought of as your friends. You can cross-sell, and do all kinds of creative things with those people. Many of them will ultimately become your very best friends.

CHAPTER TWENTY-SEVEN

"Win Your Battles"

According to the classic book The Art of War, which is often as applicable to business as it is to warfare, **"Every battle is won before you go to war."** In a sense, this is similar to that great quote from Abraham Lincoln, who once said, "If I had six hours to chop down a tree, I'd spend the first four sharpening the axe." **In other words, it's all about preparation.**

In war, the generals strategize beforehand and plot out exactly what they're going to do, and where they're going to employ their advanced weaponry. The same thing is true in business; if you plan in advance what you're going to do and, ideally, what you're prepared for, the battle will go more smoothly. If you've prepared properly, you'll be the one who wins.

So you need to win the battle of marketing before you actually do the marketing. It's all about preparation. **It's all about the things you do before you actually send your sales letter out to your marketplace, or place the ad, or whatever.** That includes attending seminars and similar events, learning to write copy, sharpening the ax with your education, and enhancing what you know about marketing. **It's knowing that effective marketing isn't just what you're going to sell to a customer the first time, but having your back-end marketing plan already in place.** Before you make the first sale, what's your second sale? Do you know that? What's your third sale? What's your entire marketing strategy? How are you going to take that person from an initial sale to a lifelong client who can be worth thousands and thousands of dollars to you?

Napoleon Bonaparte was once asked why he always seemed to know what to say, what to do, how to act. And he said, "It's because prior to every battle and prior to every major event, I spend hours meditating on all possible outcomes and consequences." **He examined all the "what if's" he could imagine, so when something did happen, he already had a framework in mind that told him exactly what to do.** That comes from the process of preparation. Why do we practice basketball? Why do football players have so many drills? <u>Because it's necessary.</u> Yes, it's hard work, but it has to be done. You may be tired of sports and military analogies by now, but we use them, because, so often, they're directly applicable to business.

Preparation is especially important. **You need to have thought through every possible aspect of how you're going to approach your marketplace and your customers.** You need to know exactly what systems to have in place to automatically lead that new prospect – that new customer – where you want them to go, so that you can maximize your profits and ultimately better serve your customer.

Preparation is something a lot of people aren't willing to do, but it's where the money is made. That's good news for you, because <u>a lot of people who enter into business are really just chasing cars</u>. They get an idea, they run off with no forethought of what happens, the project gets hard, they're out the door, and they never wind up making any money or doing anything sustaining. **The people who are really successful are those willing to devote the time, energy, and effort to preparation**. And not just preparation, but only realistic preparation. If you've read Napoleon Hill's *Think and Grow Rich*, you're aware there's something he calls "accurate thinking." **It's something a lot of people don't like, because it means you have to look at the world the way it is, not the way that you want it to be.** You have to avoid what Alan Greenspan used to call "irrational exuberance." If you're irrationally exuberant, you can't see all the things that are going to go wrong – and you need to, if only to plan for a just-in-case scenario and deal with things if they do go wrong. **If you do your due diligence and nothing goes wrong, great – you're fine. If you don't, then sure enough something bad is going to happen, and you'll be left holding the bag because you didn't prepare correctly.** This all comes back to that nasty four-letter word: work. **But that's what separates the successful people from the also-rans: the ability to sit down and focus on the nitty-gritty, the often onerous preparation, <u>because that's where the money is made</u>**. It's in the details. Chance favors the prepared mind.

At the time of this writing, there are a lot of reality shows on TV – basically, if you've seen one you've seen them all. They're kind of boring, really. But there's one new show on the market that's different: it's called "Kitchen Nightmares."

Basically, this celebrity chef named Gordon Ramsay comes into restaurants that are failing in the marketplace, and he explores all the reasons why they're failing – and then straightens them out. One week they went to a suburb of New York City and looked at a restaurant called The Mixing Bowl. **They'd been around for about 20 years, but they were just about ready to pull the plug and go out of business.** It wasn't a problem of quality; they served great food, and their kitchen was spic-and-span. One of the things Ramsay did was show them, a map of their own city as it was ten years before, with little green dots showing all the restaurants with which they competed back then. Then he showed them the same map today, with green dots for all the current competitors. <u>Little did they know that they had four times more competitors now than they had 10 years ago.</u>

It was the first time they realized this – you could tell that by their reactions on camera. In a way they were aware that there was more competition, but they were so locked into their little tiny restaurant that they forgot to realize that they needed to look outside the box sometimes. **Once they got over that shock, they decided to look at their competitors and find the gaps in the marketplace that weren't being filled.** Ramsay told them, "There's no competitor in this marketplace that's appealing to people who want to eat healthy." So they revamped the whole menu, and they found a wedge into the marketplace. It took some hard work and a lot of preparation, but they did it.

That's why I find the quote with which I started the chapter particularly relevant for business. **How are you going to prepare, to set things up, so that first of all, you can position yourself in a way that's totally different from all your competitors?** Well, first you have to look closely at all those other competitors in order to find a USP (unique selling position). Think of your company as a product on a shelf in a busy grocery store. **You have to realize there has to be something about you that's uniquely different from all the products with which you're competing.**

Aristotle Onassis once said, **"The secret to business is to know something that your competitors don't."** John Alanis told me once that one of his competitive strategies over all the other Internet marketers offering products similar to his, is simply the fact that he knows all these offline strategies that he uses to compliment his online strategies. They let him go out there and kick the competitors' butts in the marketplace. **You have to ask yourself, "What can I do? What is my strength? What do I have over the other guys?"** Once you've identified this USP, you need to find ways to strengthen it as much as possible.

Here's a good example of that. In the last chapter, I talked about how McDonald's went out there and just wiped the floor with Burger Chef. But McDonald's still has competitors, doesn't it? Burger King didn't give up the way Burger Chef did; they fought. **In fact, some say they invented the concept of the swipe file, and started to use it effectively before anyone else.** They decided they were going to go head-to-head with McDonald's, that they'd locate their stores as close to a competing McDonald's as they could, and take up the choicest locations. **They weren't afraid to face competition, and they did it creatively and successfully.** You see, in a way what the McDonald's guy did to the neighboring Burger Chef guy –- and hell, what McDonald's did that to Burger Chef in general – is what a really good poker player will sometimes do to another poker player who's less certain.

Even if the one poker player has worse cards than the other guy, he can still win if he bluffs that other guy into throwing his cards away. That said, he's got to have the resources to deal with the possibility of his bluff being called. McDonald's did have those resources, but they still won largely by bluffing. In the end, Burger Chef folded without even calling. **But look at Burger King – they called McDonald's bluff and are still around, and the competition is fierce.**

This has all turned out for the best not just for McDonald's and Burger King – both companies are doing very well – but also for the consumer. The products are more appealing to the consumer at both restaurant chains, and both have items that appeal to particular people or that are just plain better than the other guy's. Burger Chef could have stayed with it. **You don't have to be afraid of your competitors.** After all, McDonald's restaurants are franchised. **They're locked into doing certain things certain ways, and can't do the things that other outfits could have done.** Now, there's no doubt that McDonald's won over Burger Chef because they're the better company, from a business standpoint. They're probably the best in the business – but even so, there's room in the market for competition. That's my point here. <u>Don't be intimidated by the competition; look for ways that you can win in spite of it all.</u>

Don't give in to fear. **Too many people spend all their time focusing on the competition, looking for all the reasons why their competitors can win them over.** They're unable to see past the obstacles to the potential outcomes; they take little things and magnify them into big problems. While it's fine to be paranoid to some extent (as I discussed in Chapter 7), too much paranoia can hurt you, by rendering you unable to compete effectively. **Realize this: no matter what your business is, you can compete with all those other guys, if you're careful and imaginative, and are willing to work hard.** If you walk away from this book having learned that and nothing else, then I'll be happy and you'll have learned an important lesson. **You've got to have a little swagger going into the game.** <u>You can't go in feeling like you don't stand a chance – or you won't</u>.

Here's an example. Recently, a group of my friends were involved in a sporting event where our team was favored to lose. The point spread against us was eleven or twelve points, and the other team had won four out of their last five games. **But we went out there and beat them, despite the fact that our team came into the game as the underdog**. In business, you've got to have that attitude that you can win, in spite of the odds. You can't let your fears control you.

EPILOGUE

"Ruthless is as Ruthless Does"

I've know I've covered a lot of information in the past 27 chapters, and I realize you won't be able to employ all of it in your business. However, I believe that taking the basic framework of this Ruthless Marketing Attack and applying it to your business will help you reap the type of profits you've only dreamed about so far. **I know it works, because it works for me and many other entrepreneurs I know.** If we can do it, so can any other person who's willing to work hard. I hope that you'll go back again and again and reread the tips I've outlined in this book. Don't put this book on your bookshelf and let it collect dust – or you'll have wasted the wealth-making secrets of a lifetime.

When I consider why more people don't use the kinds of things I've listed here – these aggressive, assertive, proactive, offensive marketing strategies – I can think of just a few reasons. They're not good reasons, but they tend to hold most people back. First off, they're afraid of what other people are going to think. **Whenever you stick your head out there, you're taking that chance of putting it on the chopping block – and having somebody come along and whack it off.** What I'm talking about in *Ruthless Marketing Attack*! is doing things that set you apart from your competitors, things that are a little bit bold and outrageous. Often, people are simply afraid to do that.

They're also afraid, I think, for a lot of other reasons. I've talked a little about the benefits of fear. **Sometimes fear can be useful; but most of the time it's the worst thing in the world.**

It destroys our chances more than anything else. It hurts us more than it helps us. It always causes us to hold back and never take the chances that might lead to success. In Chapter 2 I told you my story, and of how my first two business partners, Gary and Dwayne, differed. **Dwayne was a nice guy, but passive. Whereas if it hadn't been for Gary Purvis, I would probably never have gotten involved in business at all. Gary was fearless. He was one of those guys who wasn't going to let anything stop him; he was going to do things no matter what.** You could give him a list of a hundred reasons why something wouldn't work and he didn't care. He'd just plow right through it all. <u>And that's the type of person you need to be, insofar as that's possible</u>. If you're not that type of person, you need to buddy-up with somebody who is, so they can supply that part of the formula to the partnership.

Fear is the destroyer of success. A lot of people let this powerful emotion hurt them more than help. Because of this they don't think big enough. As I mentioned in Chapter 15, I'd love to see the true goals of a lot of the people who are out there doing amazing things, because I know that they have them written down somewhere – and they're going for it! <u>They're not going to let fear – or anything – stop them</u>. I hope you keep that in mind and do what they do. Start getting on the other side of the cash register. **Most business owners are lousy marketers, because they're not doing much to separate themselves from everyone else to rise above all their competitors.**

Even the best of them, the savviest entrepreneurs in any field, could be doing better. But most business owners have never given a thought to trying to manage their database, or to identifying who their best customers are, or building a mailing list, and doing anything in an offensive, proactive way to do more business with their customers. <u>They're hurting themselves by not doing it</u>.

Most business owners let a lot of potential profits fly out the window. Now, it's relatively easy to save money when you're running a business. Anybody with a limited computational ability can go around and say, "Oh, let's cut this here. Let's cut here. Maybe we can save money here." **But the real money people lose is all the money that could and should be theirs, because they don't bother to develop their knowledge – to keep learning ways to ruthlessly go after that money while building value for their customers and bettering their lives.** That was the intent of this book: to give you a structure in which to operate.

Most business owners sabotage themselves by getting away from the things I've outlined in this book. Take the Smart Marketing concepts I've provided in Chapter 13 as a microcosm of this. **That process lays out step-by-step how to profit in this business.** Just about everybody I've seen who gets in trouble or isn't as successful as they should be has moved away from these things. They've violated some of the fundamentals I've outlined here. They're off chasing customers who have no long-term value whatsoever; or they're off chasing deals that don't lead to anything. **They're only trying to market on the front-end to attract new customers and they have no back-end, or they refuse to spend enough money on the front.** At the very least, I hope this book offers you guidelines for how to think about and make decisions within your business. I believe that's something most people are lacking. They're very confused; they don't know how to think.

If you put a lot of thought into the 27 powerful marketing principles we've covered in this book and use them to guide your decision-making processes, you can't help but be successful. There are so many ideas in this book that can help you make your business more profitable. **Even if you just grab one simple idea from the time you've spent reading this and apply it to your business, it's been time well-spent.** Keep this book with

---

you as you're working on your next big marketing project; flip through these pages and focus on these key ideas while you're working. Try applying them. **Make these ideas part of your business, and part of what you do.** Do it right and pretty soon, you'll be a sponge: you'll be soaked through with great ideas for your business. **Ultimately, it's a lot of fun!** I hope that's something that's come through in these pages. This entrepreneurial life is truly life on the edge at times, but it's so much fun!

I wish you that type of success and fun in your life, and in parting, I want to tell you this: <u>don't forget to treat all aspects of business and marketing as if it is a game</u>. Don't even think about it as business; don't think about it as work. Think about it as a game. **You're playing to win, and the goal is to make as much money as you can, as fast as you can, while having fun!** Be ruthless, be relentless and aggressive, but be ethical. Do everything in the best possible way. And yet, go out there to make as much money as possible as fast as you can.

Do whatever makes you feel most alive!

www.ingramcontent.com/pod-product-compliance
Lightning Source LLC
Chambersburg PA
CBHW031401180326
41458CB00043B/6566/J